What Ross calls 'mental gymnastics,' I call liberation work. This book is essential for anyone overcoming personal or systemic odds.

Trissa Tismal-Capili | USA Today and Wall Street Journal Bestselling Author, and Founder, Institute of Conscious Business Leaders

This isn't just about learning a new process; it's about shifting your mentality. *Mastering the TPS Blueprint* is your roadmap to conquering your mind and breaking through barriers.

Casel Burnett | Vice President, LODI, and International Bestselling Author of *No Regrets*

Rewriting your mental story is hard work, but in *Mastering the TPS Blueprint*, Ross lays out exactly how to take actionable steps toward success.

Tamara Nall | CEO & Founder, The Leading Niche

Ross delivers a masterclass in mental endurance and strategic success—this book is required reading for any leader aiming to build an unstoppable organization from the inside out.

Aaron Poynton | Author, *Think Like A Black Sheep*

This isn't just a book—it's a mental training ground. Ross rewires the reader's relationship with failure and discipline like no one else.

Brandon Blewett | Author, *How to Avoid Strangers on Airplanes*

If you're looking to turn your business vision into tangible, scalable results, *Mastering the TPS Blueprint* by Darius Ross delivers the no-nonsense framework you've been waiting for. Packed with practical insights and real-world applications, this book is a masterclass in building sustainable wealth and achieving personal excellence. It's a powerful read for serious entrepreneurs ready to move from idea to impact.

Carl Grant, III | Author of *How to Live the Abundant Life*

Mastering the TPS Blueprint

Transforming Trauma Into Triumph

DARIUS ALEXANDER "DMAN" ROSS

ISBN **979-8-9987130-0-2** (pbk)
ISBN **979-8-9987130-1-9** (hcv)
ISBN **979-8-9987130-2-6** (ebook)

Library of Congress Control Number: **2025908398**

Contents

Dedication

To Malachi and Alice Ross
My parents, thanks for never stopping the mailman delivering thousands of my books and magazines for years, and for all the lessons learned and unlearned! Smiles!

To my grandparents
From both sides and all my ancestral relatives all the way to Pharoah Ramses III.

To my "mini mes," Alexander and Tmia
This is Dad's book therapy.

To my Aunt Mattie
My harshest critic, who pushed me to master speaking and to learn the power of words and the English language!

To my ancestors
From Nigeria, India, Bangladesh, Sri Lanka, China, the rest of the Asian continent, and the South American continent—my ancestral brothers and sisters!

To the teachers who helped create and craft my life's journeys
Mrs. Early (1st grade); Mrs. Barbara Kaufman (4th grade); Mrs. Dorothy Williams (7th grade); Mrs. Porter, Mrs. Cindy Thomas and Sister Elvira (8th grade).

Mr. Hana; Mrs. Varovodic; Dr. Lopez; Father Cain; Father Mike Pflegher; Coach Bonk.

And, in my profession: Marty Farmer; Susan Gordy; Billy Rapp; E. Bronfman; W. McDonough.

To all the ladies in my personal and intimate life who helped shape these insights into the pros and cons of human behavior
LDK; JMA; EH; RVG; RR; SB; LMD; LJ; AC

Thank you for giving me insights into loving women in a raw and unfiltered way. What a journey it's been!

Acknowledgements

Special thanks to my writing coach and mentor, Phoenix Roberts—without whom this book could not have been completed.

A heartfelt thank you to the team at Leaders Brands for their exceptional work in completing this project. I am deeply grateful for their dedication and expertise. I also give thanks to God for blessing me with the strength to maintain, sustain, and prosper through 59 years of transformation and transition.

Preface: An Allegory

Hollywood movies often advertise themselves as being "inspired by true events." I wanted to begin this book by explaining exactly why I wrote it—but I couldn't figure out how to do so. Just before the manuscript was finished, I had an idea. I shared it with my writing coach, and he kindly put together the following, brought together from the real experiences of a number of persons:

"I Dreamed a Dream"

My beloved grandchildren,

My doctor tells me it's almost time for me to go but, before I do, I want to share an experience I had a few years ago, when I was struggling with this whole "mortality" thing.

I dreamed a dream.

In this vision, I somehow knew that I was in the presence of our Lord and Savior. Though I could neither see Him nor hear Him directly, He somehow spoke to my mind and heart. I knelt by the Throne, and wept with a mixture of love and despair, my mind filled with one question, "Why, Lord, did it have to hurt so much?"

I felt His smile of love and understanding. "Tell me, little brother," my mind said.

Daddy abandoned us. He cheated on momma. When she found out, she lost her respect for him. So, he told me, "When a man loses the respect of his wife, he is no longer The Man. It's done. Now, you are The Man, so take care of your mother," and he just walked out on us.

"And when he did," my mind answered, "you stepped up. You became the man your mother needed you to be. What else?"

A few years later, someone threatened to kill me because I dated a woman he wanted. He can't do that, but I knew he would. I was sure he would. So I ran.

"And you chose a new city, where you became a man of success, a spokesman for your industry, a rebuilder of communities. What else?"

That work took over my life; every hour, my mind was filled with that next deal, the deal I had to make happen. It was too much to handle, and I drank. I got really lost for a while.

"But, only for a time. And, now, you sponsor others and help them rebuild their lives. What else?"

But it hurt, the healing as much as the addiction. It hurt so much I couldn't deal with it. I was so unhappy, life seemed so hopeless... I almost ended it just so the pain would stop.

"But you didn't. What you suffered and overcame gave you strength. Not just to help others, but to understand that whatever comes in life, it shall be but for a small moment. And when the Enemy said, 'You can't make it, give up,' you told him, 'I can!' and you didn't give up."

You did all this to me to teach me?

"Oh, no, your pains came when you or others chose badly. But when others plant bad seeds, I can harvest good fruits, when My brothers and sisters let me. Like Mine other servants, I chose thee in the furnace of thine afflictions. We knew your potential—and that you needed tempering—softening to the sufferings of others and toughening so you had strength enough to share.

"And, when that strength was needed, you shared freely. Keep sharing, thou good and faithful servant. In the end, a place awaits thee."

And I awoke.

I have tried, children, and, now that I'm going, I bequeath that challenge to you.

With all my love,
Grandpa

The TPS Blueprint

The book is based on something I've seen in numerous individuals, including myself:

We're so intent on taking care of our routines that we regularly miss the mark. We miss many of the ideal situations that can truly advance our lives.

The Three Legs of the Stool

Anyone who has ever sat on a three-legged stool knows that it's generally more stable than a four-legged chair. Even the best chairs can have small differences in leg length, giving the chair a slight wobble. Even the least expensive stool sits stable—that is a fundamental of mathematics, that three points define a plane.

This book focuses on how the three points of the TPS Blueprint—**timing, precision,** and **synchronicity**—can lead you to success and impact every aspect of your life positively, but only if all three aspects are used cooperatively. Before we get started, therefore, a clear definition of TPS is necessary:

Timing

Business timing is all about predicting customer needs and meeting them. Bringing the right products to market when there is high demand requires in-depth and impartial research.

We often hear *Carpe diem!*—"Seize the day!" It's a valuable attitude because, as I mentioned, too many of us don't, and we end up missing the moment and whatever advantages it might present.

However, *Carpe diem!* actually has two parts: The first—and perhaps most difficult—is recognizing the moment. The second is seizing the moment by deciding to act on it.

You may have heard the old saying, "Failure to decide plus time equals a decision." So very true. We are constantly bombarded with opportunities to choose. Most of those choices have a time limit attached. Ultimately, the clock runs out, the moment of choice passes and, if we fail to decide, we miss the mark.

A simple example: We all have a natural rhythm in our moods and energy levels. Studies suggest that people's moods tend to rise in the morning, dip in the afternoon, and rise again in the evening until just before bedtime. For this reason, some researchers suggest you avoid making important decisions or taking tests late in the day. When you are less energetic and happy, you might have trouble getting to the right answer.

On the other hand, if you need to solve problems that entail insight rather than logic, the afternoon may be better for the opposite reason. Being less focused might leave your mind more open to making more creative leaps.

We should tackle important tasks during our personal peak hours.

Timing also determines a hefty part of your results because only you understand the factors that influence a given decision or the course of action you might undertake. These change over time.

For example, you're thriving in your current job when an opportunity with another company presents itself—more money, a bigger office, a better title. The inducements to take the job could be as numerous as they are desirable. However, you're in the middle of a long-term project which you helped initiate. Is it fair to jump ship on your teammates? Perhaps, instead, you decided to join your current company because of the learning opportunities it presented. Have you learned everything these people can teach you? Would the new job require moving to a new city? How would that affect your family?

These and other factors will go into the decision to stay in your present position or move on. Those factors could be many, and they could be confusing. The choice between something good and something bad is easy. The choice between two good options is, frequently, not easy at all. So, I ask you:

Is today the day to seize?

Precision

Precision is not the same as accuracy. Accuracy concerns reaching a desired result, staying within predetermined parameters, or maintaining predetermined standards. Precision goes beyond that.

Let's look at a military example: The Roman legions had a trick called "the turtle." Legionaries interlocked their shields to form a protective shell against the enemy—some holding them above their heads, others to the left or right, and still others in front or behind. As a result, they were protected from enemy spears and arrows on all sides, except their feet. They could get in among the enemy without casualties and really mess up the enemy's formation, if, and I cannot stress this enough, and only if every soldier inside the turtle held position. One legionnaire off his mark by even a foot or two could create a gap in the turtle's shell. Put a couple of spears through that gap, injure or kill just one or two soldiers, and the turtle's integrity is compromised.

A modern example would be line dancing: everybody has to be in straight lines, and everybody has to perform the same steps and turn at the same time. If the dancers don't move in sync, everybody will be tripping over everybody else's feet! Definitely not the way to impress.

Precision is accuracy plus consistency. It's getting the result you plan for every time, with a minimum of errors. You may have heard the old carpenter's saw (pun intended): "Measure twice, cut once." Precision is knowing the right way to do something and doing it the right way every time. (And it should be noted, the more people involved in an operation, the greater your chances of failure if a single person acts imprecisely.) Living a life of precision helps you maintain focus and motivation towards constant improvement.

How Important Is Precision for You as an Entrepreneur?

Many people believe there is a fine line between success and failure, and I agree wholeheartedly. In fact, precision is often the difference that makes the difference. As you work to build a reputation for quality products or services, a perfectionist mindset can markedly improve your chances of success.

In this usage, "perfect" doesn't mean "flawless." (No shocker there, I hope.) We're human, we make mistakes, and the wise among us build the inevitability of mistakes into our plans. The questions arise: How many mistakes are "acceptable"? What kind of mistakes are "acceptable"? How often can mistakes be "acceptable"? Best to decide this up front so you're not making it up as you go along with regard to errors because you may not have time for a long debate over mistakes.

How Does Precision Work in Business?

Being precise starts with an idea that most of us learn during our first year of work. Small things or small attitude changes can increase your chances of stepping up and getting the job done despite limited working experience.

It starts with organization. Understand what your employer expects of you. Plan your day. Use your calendar app or other tools. Bring a pen and paper to staff meetings and take notes. This demonstrates interest and helps you keep track of projects and expectations as they change. When given an assignment, write it down in detail. This might not seem like much in the moment but as the old proverb goes, "The weakest pencil is mightier than the strongest memory." On your own, you're likely to forget a small thing which could cost you the trust of your superiors.

Taking notes is also an effective method of keeping your work attached to the common thread, central theme, or governing principle of a project. Being precise, having an eye for detail, paying attention to what's going on—it all makes you stand out from the pack.

Synchronicity

Carl Jung, the famous psychologist, coined the term "synchronicity," most often defined as "the meaningful connection between the subjective and objective world."[1] In a simpler term, it's often called **life's mysterious coincidences**. Synchronicity happens when events come together at times where everything seems to be in stroke, where events pile up with precision, or when things seem "too good to be true."

Some simple examples:

You're talking with a friend about a loved one you haven't heard from in a while and, without warning, they show up before the end of the conversation. When such things happen, we often say, jokingly, "Speak of the devil, and he appears!"

While shopping in a supermarket, you see an individual you hold as a role model or admire in some other way, perhaps someone you've read about or seen on TV. You walk towards them to introduce yourself and tell them what a positive influence they've had on your life. Suddenly, you decide to turn back, embarrassed about intruding their privacy. As you turn, however, you see a Nike sports bag emblazoned with the Nike motto, "Just do it." Coincidence? Maybe yes, maybe no, but it encourages you. You turn back again and make the connection.

Synchronicity is an interesting and much-debated concept. Could the subconscious mind be the cause? Could God be arranging events for some divine purpose? Could it be a combination of natural energies? Could it be pure coincidence? Could it be plain, dumb luck?

---

[1] Very commonly quoted but not found among his writings. It's probably a summary of an actual Jung writing, "We shall naturally look round in vain the macro physical world for acausal events, for the simple reason that we cannot imagine events that are connected non-causally and are capable of a non-causal explanation. But that does not mean that such events do not exist... The so-called 'scientific view of the world' based on this [idea] can hardly be anything more than a psychologically biased partial view which misses out all those by no means unimportant aspects that cannot be grasped statistically." Jung, Carl Gustav. *Synchronicity: An Acausal Connecting Principle*. Princeton NJ: Princeton University Press, 1960.

Yes, to all of the above.

For whatever reason, synchronicity happens, and, frankly, we just accept it because we can't do anything else. It's nice to have a few mysteries in life.

On the other hand, police and military personnel are taught to "keep your head on a swivel," which means to be aware of your situation. Awareness breeds control because it sees opportunities, generally before others do. Does that mysterious thing we call "coincidence" mean our subconscious is blending our experience and our corner-of-the-eye awareness? Most times, we assume it's just some unplanned opportunity. Perhaps, instead, it is (at least, sometimes) one soul reaching out and touching another soul with a similar energy.

Having developed the skills of timing and precision, it may be that your readiness for a new opportunity becomes subconsciously obvious to another who has a new opportunity waiting for the right person.

Why Did I Write this Book? To Whom did I write It?

I'm writing to an audience that's going through the same things that I went through.

They're trying to discover where they went wrong.

- First, I'm writing to the 18- to 24-year-olds (those recently out of high school or college) who are just beginning their working careers and adult lives. They have bright eyes and bushy tails, believing everything's going be perfectly on point. This is because they haven't really seen or carefully listened to elder wisdom.

- Second, I'm writing to those in the middle of life (20-somethings to 40-somethings) who are saying, "Oh, I've made few mistakes, but I've got plenty of time left to fix them." They don't realize that the clock is ticking, and none of us have as much time as we think. In fact, more and more people are learning just how little time one life can have.

- Finally, I'm writing to those in the latter part of mortality. Reaching 50 isn't what it used to be. We're not beginning to be old at that age anymore. In fact, some of us are really just coming into our own. If they've gotten this far, they still have a chance to make significant adjustments and create a better future that might be 40 years long, or even more. Still, some won't make the needed adjustments because fear has set in and they're apprehensive because of what's already happened in their lives.

This is my version of that personal guide. I hope you find it useful in writing yours.

CHAPTER 2

Mental Gymnastics and Peak Performance

For whatever reason, and opinions vary widely, we are programmed to fail.

To a point.

Sometimes, failure is inevitable because we lack the skills and experience to complete the task at hand. (More on this later.) Most of the time, failure is not inevitable because we have, but don't employ, all the skills of all the people who could help make a project successful.

Discipline Beats Motivation

Those of us who are old enough to remember the 1984 Summer Olympics in Los Angeles, California, should remember a little girl named Mary Lou Retton. At just sixteen years old and standing only four feet and nine inches tall, she was the star of the Games. As always, women's gymnastics were a highlight of the event, and the competition was fierce. With two events to go, Retton was second in the overall women's competition by just 0.15 points. Her last event was the vault. In that competition, the athletes run towards a horse-shaped standard and vault over it, spinning and turning and landing on a mat. As Retton stood at the starting edge of the runway, the cameras focused on her face as she readied herself for her win-or-lose it all moment. While perfect scores (10 out of 10) weren't unknown, they were still rare, but spectators remember Retton's expression—absolute focus, pure determination. Many knew what was about to happen. The tiny teen ran, hit the springboard, vaulted over the horse, and "stuck the landing" like few ever had.

The crowd went wild, the judges had no choice, the scoreboard lit up with that perfect 10.0, and Retton won the gold medal by a razor-thin 0.05 points, becoming the first American woman gymnast to be the Olympic all-around champion.

Inspired by Nadia Comaneci and the first perfect 10 in Olympic history (1972 in Munich, Germany), Retton dedicated twelve years to daily practice of her sport. She was at a physical peak that few will ever achieve but, looking at her face before that fateful vault, it's clear that her mental discipline was as important, if not more important, than her physical skills or motivation.

"I want the gold," is every Olympian's motivation. Such a win is as close to the immortality of the ancient Greek gods as any modern mortal can aspire to achieve. Likewise, their skills are so close to equal that, if they were stones, you couldn't slide a knife between them. When all is said and done, it is the mind that can ignore all distractions—from your place on the tote board to the cheers of the crowd to the fact that you had knee surgery just five weeks ago—and take the crown.

Failure vs. Determination

All of us are born into an imperfect world—into environments with toxic elements. How much does this contribute to a failure mindset?

I think it's an even split, 50 percent of failure is environmental and 50 percent is behavioral. I wrote an essay about adversity for an anthology, where I suggested that too many kids today are spoiled. Parents have an obligation to protect their children but only from things the children can't protect themselves against. As we grow, we become more able, and we should be required to deal with more and more of our problems.

In this regard, my kids sometimes have a problem with me. They've been heard to say, "Dad sure is tough on us." Yes, I am. Even though they're now adults, I'm still teaching them to survive in the 21st century, which grows more challenging every day. When they give me grief over it, I remind them, "Both of you are surviving. No matter what the circumstances are, you can figure it out."

Failure as a Product of Attitude

Some children are raised by parents who have the resources to protect their children from the consequences of their childish actions. This rarely ends well. Another example:

25

"The Alexander brothers—Alon, Oren, and Tal—have been arrested on federal sex trafficking charges, according to New York prosecutors.

For well over a decade, the prominent real estate brothers conspired to 'repeatedly and violently drug, sexually assault and rape dozens of women,' according to an indictment unsealed Wednesday in New York after the brothers were arrested in Miami on Wednesday.

'At times, the Alexander brothers arranged for these sexual assaults well in advance, using the promise of luxury experiences, travel, and accommodations to lure and entice women to locations where they were then forcibly raped or sexually assaulted, sometimes by multiple men, including one or more of the Alexander brothers,' the indictment said."[2]

How did this happen? Either they were never taught proper respect towards women or they somehow came to believe no one could touch them because of their wealth. (Alon and Oren hold the record for the single largest residential purchase in history—almost $240 million for a Manhattan condo.)

Some children—Dr. McNair, I think, was one such child—learn proper behaviors. In general terms, their thinking can be summed up as, "We cannot do this because this is unacceptable among civilized people, and we are civilized people." They wouldn't commit that crime in the first place.

However, other children learned that actions have consequences and when they get caught misbehaving the first or

---

[2] Katersky, Aaron, Julia Reinstein, and Victoria Arancio. 2024. "Real estate tycoons the Alexander brothers arrested on federal sex trafficking charges," *ABC News.*, 11 December. https://abcnews.go.com/US/real-estate-tycoons-alexander-brothers-arrested-federal-charges/story?id=116680590, accessed 31 January 2025.

second time, their thinking runs something like, "We did this and we suffered punishment because of what we did. We don't like the punishment; therefore, we won't do that again." They don't become repeat offenders.

A few, like the Alexander brothers, seem to have learned, "We're rich, we're untouchable, we can buy our way out of anything." They become monsters.

Legal proceedings are ongoing as I write this book, so, the future will tell us how touchable the Alexander boys actually were.

Your Head Can Do a Number on You

Happiness—what does this condition really depend on? Is it something that's found by chance or is it a design of fate?

Does happiness depend solely on our bank account? Absolutely not. Are the lottery mega-winners happy? No, most go broke within five years because their wealth wasn't earned, meaning they didn't value it properly, and most end up wasting it on self-indulgent "toys." Even many of those who have earned "wealthy" levels of success are not happy because they just end up accumulating more "stuff."

Happiness is an emotional state and most people understand that. Our emotional intelligence (EI) is our ability to deal with our own emotions and those of others. Developing an EI tool kit (that is, a set of attitudes and actions by which we deal with other people) includes self-awareness, self-regulation, empathy, compassion, and social skills. It also enhances our relationships. Happy relationships—a loving family, close friendships, respect from coworkers and employers, self-approbation,[3] and so on—contribute to a happy life. I would suggest, in fact, that the happiest people are those with the happiest relationships (a high EI) and the largest number of them. The unhappiest people are those with an unhappy mindset (and low EI) which lead to unhappy relationships and fewer relationships overall.

Your mindset is your perception of your reality, and your perception will lead you to live in what you see as a very happy or unhappy reality. Those who perceive an unhappy reality can perceive an unhappy mindset in others (whether it exists or not) which leads to misperceptions about your world that can ruin your relationships and your happiness. An analogy:

The Earth is basically divided into three parts—a solid core, a fluid mantle, and a solid surface. I suggest that humans are similar:

• We have core needs which drive us to seek relationships and interaction with others.

• We wear a mantle (a cloak or overcoat) of activities or attitudes that the world sees and to which they react.

• We present a public face, our surface, that people respond to positively or negatively, based on their perception of our activities or attitudes.

The Core

***To be happy, you must first understand
what you need and what defines you.***

---

[3] Self-approbation, noun, "the quality or feeling of being very pleased with yourself." (Adapted from "Self-approbation," *dictionary.cambridge.org*. Cambridge, UK: Cambridge University Press & Assessment, 2025. https://dictionary.cambridge.org/us/dictionary/english/self-approbation, accessed 30 January 2025.)

If you get those two points, there's little chance you'll end up among those people who wander aimlessly through life with an empty heart. Knowledge of our needs, as opposed to our wants, and understanding the limits we put on our behavior, are the keys to being happy.

What Do You Need?

Most people would put air, water, food, clothing, or shelter at the top of the list. That's true, but only for physical survival, the lowest rung on Maslow's famous "Hierarchy of Needs."

> You can get everything in life you want if you will just help enough other people get what they want.
>
> –Zig Ziglar, *Secrets of Closing the Sale*, 1984.

To achieve the highest level, which Maslow calls "self-actualization"–to become the best person you can be–you need to contribute something to the world. Remember, you never know what kind of change your "small" contribution to another will create. You can make the world a better place so that everyone, you included, will appreciate the fact that you lived here.

What Defines You?

What do you choose as your definition? Perhaps:

I'm a man. I'm an African-American. I'm a citizen of the United States. I'm a business owner. I'm a pundit.

No, these are descriptions of me, not my definitions. They say something about me, but they don't fully tell the world who I am. A "man" may be many things, a "citizen" may hold a variety of values, a "pundit" might be wise or a complete fool.

I am a Christian.

That is a definition because it says I have adopted and live by a known code of thought and behavior. You can predict my actions in a situation because there are imperatives that drive me which outweigh all other considerations and limits beyond which I won't pass.

My definition is religious; yours might be political or philosophical or ethical, it doesn't matter. What matters is that you are committed to this or that course of action and everybody knows it.

In business, charities, and other organizations, we call these vision statements. My vision, as a Christian, is returning home to the God who gave me life. Whatever your vision is, it's the long-term goal of your existence. Without it, you cannot control your life experience any more than a traveler in a strange area can find his destination without a map.

The Mantle

Next, let's look at a direct extension of our core to the fundamental pillar of emotional intelligence:

> ***To be happy, you must have good
> relationships with others;
> to do that, you must first have a good
> relationship with yourself.***

A woman—thanks to her technical skills, her dedication, and the fact that she took advantage of her opportunities—has reached a position of leadership in her industry. Despite this success, she isn't happy. She has a fancy car and a big house, takes vacations all over the world, and is, by every measure the world has, living "the good life." She, however, feels an existential emptiness—a restlessness not fulfilled by the material goods she's accumulated nor by her relationships with others.

Realizing this, she takes the reins of her life and dives into her inner self. She asks hard questions and finds hard answers:

- She chose to rise quickly by showing others the great things she could do.

- Her actions were designed to publicly outdo everyone else in her sphere.

- She only maintained relationships with those who could help her advance.

- She worked hard to impress others, to assert herself in front of coworkers, to show off her greatness.

- If anyone outshined her, she sabotaged their successes.

What a bitch! (Pardon my language, but I know you were also thinking it.) As a result of these choices, she has no close friends or family members. She has everything the world offers, yet it isn't enough.

The Surface

The woman in this example presented a public face no one liked. She realized this after much self-reflection. She also realized that she didn't even like the person she'd become. She achieved the goal she set for herself early in life, but the victory was empty because she had no one to share it with. No one wants to be an intimate part of her life.

It's our dissatisfaction with the path we're on that pushes us to do better. Occasionally, that means forcing ourselves off the path we've chosen because it isn't the path to success, meaning happiness. Sometimes, we take the wrong path because that's what others expect or because we're afraid to leave our comfort zone, or for some other silly reason. In doing that, we turn our backs on the inner voice that's desperate to be heard, because it knows where our ultimate happiness can be found.

Self-approbation, which I mentioned earlier, is about being satisfied with ourselves—being our own best friend, as people used to say. People who don't like themselves are seldom fun to be around, so they can't build strong, positive relationships with others. Let's face it: if it's obvious you don't like yourself—well, you know yourself best. If you have reasons to dislike yourself, we'll trust your judgment and not like you either.

But the good news is: all of that can change. Self-respect is based on this self-knowledge. When we know we've changed, others will eventually see it, too.

One final thought: Happiness is not an accumulation of "things"—including knowledge, honors, and other intangibles. The happiest person isn't the one who has or knows the most, but the one who understands the most. An old sage once said, "The smartest man in the room is the one who knows what he knows (which is much) and knows what he does not know (which is much more)." Humility is an undervalued personality trait. Humility allows us—maybe even forces us—to ask those hard questions and listen to those hard answers. It enables us to say, "I don't know it all, and I don't need to be the best."

That is the beginning of wisdom.

CHAPTER 3

Why Your Mind Loves Mediocrity

Unrealistic Goals

Lowballing Yourself

Shoot for the stars, you might land on the roof.
Shoot for the roof, you might land in the trash can.

–Modern Proverb

It's true, and we, as a society, have been saying and hearing things like this for generations. Modern America was built on accomplishments by people who, as a friend of mine likes to say, tongue-in-cheek, "They were too dumb to know that it couldn't be done, so, they went out and did it." We owe those thickheads a debt of gratitude.

However–and this is a big "however"–when do we talk about setting the bar too low? We hear that goals should be challenging, and I agree wholeheartedly, but I'm not talking about quarterly or yearly sales metrics, or whatever it is you use to measure success. I'm talking about your legacy. What do you want to be remembered for when you "shuffle off this mortal coil," as Shakespeare said?[4]

Let's start with the smartest kid in the class–the one who always raises their hand and knows the answer to every question. There are usually other things involved beyond just having a higher IQ than anyone else in the room–but smart people often pay a price. They might be on the autism spectrum. They might be introverted. They might be a number of things. Whatever the case, bullies–and every school has them–abuse them because they can get away with it. Smart kids generally aren't the ones who fight back, so they just take it.

But, suppose they do more than just take the abuse. Suppose that they stop raising their hands. They become the quiet kid in the back of the room. They get the grades but don't interact with others. They never really fit in before but now, they're almost non-existent. We might call this "the shadow syndrome." They may spend their lives in those shadows never contributing what they could to society because they fear the consequences.

Alternatively, they might become class clowns. As I've said, many of our smartest kids have limited social skills, which invites the attention they don't want. So, they try to attract attention they do want. They see what happens to others and they attach themselves to the "cool" kids with entertainment. Hiding their talents and making fools of themselves is

---

[4] Shakespeare, William. *Hamlet* (Act III, Scene 1), circa 1600.

the price they pay for acceptance. In doing so, they learn that what they have to offer the world isn't highly valued. We might call this "the jester syndrome."

Either way, they learn to not stand out because of their abilities—being outstanding out means inviting mistreatment. They become mental mediocrities because it's safe.

In another example, from my own life—and I have to start by saying this is my experience only, with some of the women I've known, I'm not suggesting this is universal:

I've dated many wonderful Latina women, some of whom end up selling themselves short. They came to America for a better life. Some feel they had to leave a child behind with family, so they don't expose their child to the risks of a new country, language, culture, and so on. These women then send money back home to support their child and help their families generally.

Here's the problem: when they get to America, some say to themselves, "I have to do everything I can for the family because I left my child behind with them." That's a perfectly reasonable and responsible attitude. However, some families abuse that willingness to assist, and these immigrants end up taking care of their whole family in the old country. Even though they could support themselves, they live off the immigrant's labor. The immigrants struggle to earn a better life while the money they send back home provides a very comfortable life for their relatives.

At some point, these women should get their child to join them then tell the families to get off their backs. They don't because they feel beholden or indebted to their relatives. They lose the motivation to improve themselves because they won't profit from that extra work. It's as if they're waiting for someone in the family to pardon them for leaving home to build a better life. The family is punishing them for being successful. This is something I've never understood. I'm guessing some kind of a guilt trip is involved, but it's more than just a guilt trip. Those families know better, but they refuse to recognize the problem and do better.

Along this same line, I assume all of you have known women in business and some of you have seen them suffering from "the imposter syndrome." Essentially, when a woman walks into a board room or after she's been promoted to an executive position, she starts thinking, "I don't belong here." That's not true, you earned that position. Those jobs aren't handed out at random—or because you're nice looking. Stockholders and managers hoard those jobs because they are valuable and come with power—power that, if used incompetently, could ruin a company. Those who pass judgement on those jobs decided that you **do** belong there. Accept their judgement of you, thank them for the opportunity, then get to work—show them how you're worth even more than they give you credit for!

This situation I described with the immigrants is the imposter syndrome, just in another direction. Instead of, "I'm here but I don't deserve to be," some people get it into their heads that "In my country, there are expectations. I come here but I must respect that culture, I must be what my culture says I should be." They become trapped in expectations because they are all they know. They live as imposters because they hold themselves down to those expectations.

The freedom of immigration to a new culture is the freedom to set your own expectations. Instead, they end up pimping themselves into a mediocre life, even though most could do better. Like "the imposter syndrome," these women (it also happens to men, but in smaller numbers) have let others judge their value or worth or destiny.

The Destiny Realm

Speaking of destiny, there's another set of unrealistic goals—not the ones that are too high or too low, but ones that veer too far to the left or right. They're not out of reach—they're just off course.

> If I may be so bold, it was a mistake for you to accept promotion. Commanding a starship is your first, best destiny; anything else is a waste of material.
>
> —"Mister Spock" (Leonard Nimoy)[5]

In my 20s, I became somewhat successful in real estate in Chicago. When circumstances forced me to move, I chose New York. The market seemed ripe (the timing was good) and I had the skills (I was precise), so I continued working in real estate and, again, became successful. I was content to keep doing that when synchronicity came into play—and not for the first time, but that is a story for later.

I set my goal, and, I think, a very realistic one, to become the biggest real estate mogul around. It didn't quite work out that way.

This was during the Bush Administration, when significant changes were made to the estate tax laws. A group I belonged to needed a spokesperson and despite a lack of experience in this arena, I was chosen. I dove in, and within a short time, 1,500 different media outlets were interviewing me. Suddenly, I found myself at the center of a lot of unexpected attention. Shortly after the estate tax excitement died down, a new minimum wage law was proposed for New York and, again, I found myself as a spokesperson. I eventually realized that real estate wasn't going to be my main career. I became a pundit, and everything that I did was connected to the minimum wage law, the estate tax law, or something that had to do with economics. You could say I became an urban economist.

---

[5] Meyer, Nicholas, director. *Star Trek II: The Wrath of Khan*. Paramount Pictures Corporation, 1982.

I saw the winds changing and reset my sails. My work as a commentator led to having a platform which then led into the buying of businesses and my new career in acquisitions and, later, venture capital. I completely left real estate to play that new game. It was an interesting sequence of events, starting with some that nothing to do with me. A door opened—not a door that I opened or one I wanted opened, but, when I saw the opportunity, I thought to myself, "I can get in here."

At the same time, social media was also rising fast—booming—in fact, after the World Wide Web came along in 1991. Quickly, some people realized that more opportunities were opening up almost every year. Along the way, it steadily grew as a place for open communications, so, I communicated. It all worked out better than expected. By the time YouTube came along in 2005, I was seen everywhere I wanted to be seen.

None of that would have happened had I stuck to real estate and tried to become the big man on campus. My previous goal, realistic at the time I set it, ceased to be realistic. Could I overtake against Donald Trump, who'd become the big name in New York real estate (and other things) in the 1990s? No, that wasn't going to happen. He had more money and connections. I was outmatched.

How does my synchronicity theory fit into all this? I was somewhat in the "Fake it 'til you make it," mode of thinking. I was thinking about what I wanted to do, not about what I should have been doing. I have no idea what my "first, best destiny" could be.

I don't, by the way, blame myself for not knowing my destiny. Very few people have the right vision for their lives until they've lived a good portion of it. There are those who honestly say, "I knew I wanted to be a [whatever] since I was a kid," and they end up being an exceptional [whatever]—doctor, pilot, diesel mechanic, rancher. I admire their vision and self-awareness. I had to be presented with an unforeseen opportunity before I became aware.

I wanted to be a real estate magnate, but when I saw another opportunity that could help my business, by becoming a social and philanthropic activist. It didn't. Instead, it turned my life in a whole new direction. Eventually, I realized that what I envisioned was never realistic because my personality, training, experience, and entire being naturally suited me for something else. I realized that I could make my mark and have a more positive effect on the community elsewhere.

People were listening to me, so, I thought, let's roll with what's working and forget what's not working: this will get me what I want, which will get me business deals—and those deals will bring all the other things I'm after. This book is part of that process and, if this helps you get what you want, it's part of your process as well.

The Key to the Equation

If you can't get any traction on any goals that you've set, then you've got to turn around and go where you get traction.

That's the key.

In writing this book, I worked with a wonderful coach. We didn't intend for his story to become part of mine but, on this subject and a couple of others, his story parallelled mine.

He graduated from a good university with a degree in film production—because they actually made movies on film way back then! Unfortunately, where he lived, the timing was bad for motion picture production when he graduated. Fortunately, one of the most respected filmmakers in his area needed an apprentice because he was overworked. Coach said, "Well it's not exactly my line, but I'll spread the word." Coach had that one shot at a movie career, and he missed the target completely. It was a moment of synchronicity, and he walked away without even trying. Why? "Because," he later said, "I didn't know enough to know that I didn't know enough." That apprenticeship would've taught him vital skills and introduced him to all the right people. He didn't know that fact, so he passed on it.

He later became a writer for an e-commerce company. This was the beginning of the search engine optimization revolution, and his employer was at the forefront. When they parted, he made a critical mistake. Had he realized he was witnessing the infancy of a new industry, he might've realized that he was at the forefront of it. In this case, the timing was right, the synchronicity was there—but the precision just wasn't there.

Coach loved writing but didn't fancy the technical research work required for SEO—the information that made the writing commercially valuable. Therefore, he didn't learn what he'd need to know to become an SEO guru. He became a very underemployed copywriter for a long and ever-changing list of clients. He never got traction as a copywriter and, therefore, never found the traction he needed for real success.

Happily, he has found a niche where he gets a lot of traction—where all three factors aligned. Today, he has a global clientele. He's mentoring people to create best-selling books that help people advance their lives and careers. He's enjoying a very comfortable, living in a happy semi-retirement life.

Other examples include Bill Gates, who saw the infancy of the home computer—and jumped in; Steve Chen, Chad Hurley, and Jawed Karim, who saw the potential of a platform to share videos and created YouTube; and Mark Zuckerberg and a few friends, who saw the possibility of replacing letters to individuals with short notes to the entire world—and Facebook was born.

As I noted in chapter one:

- There are two parts to timing: The first is recognizing the moment, and the second is seizing it. Miss either one, and you'll be left wondering what might have been.

- Being precise is not possible if you lack the necessary skills. If you don't have the skills, you must acquire them or try something else.

- When all the stars align and your moment comes, you need to go! Don't wait, don't hesitate, don't overthink the question, get moving and take action!

Keep a Weather Eye Out

That old sailor's phrase wasn't just good advice; for ships at sea in the old days, the weather meant life or death. A bad storm could wreck you in an instant, so sailors watched the horizon carefully for any changes.

Today, that principle remains good advice.

I was talking recently to someone about the economy. I said, "I consider myself an urban economist. If you go out and look around to see what's going on, you'll recognize things are changing. Where there is change, there is opportunity."

I cannot stress enough the importance of seeing what's happening around you and recognizing its significance to you. Take New York City—if you walk with your gaze straight ahead, all you'll see are the things at street level. But, if you look up, you'll see all these high-rise buildings. Like everything else, somebody owns them. It could be an individual, a few families, or a corporation. Somebody's making thousands—if not millions or billions—of dollars from those buildings.

If you never look up, you will never see it. If you don't take yourselves out of your own little environment and look around, you'll never see what problems exist and you'll never get paid for finding a solution.

I've often thought that the key difference between being rich and poor is this: A rich person focuses on other people's problems and asks, "Well, how can I fix this?" A poor person, on the other hand, focuses on their own problems and thinks, "I've got to keep hustling and grinding or this problem will drag me under."

By the way, does a CEO do the accounting? Do they change the toilet paper or open the lobby doors? Sort and deliver the mail?

- to understand the vision and mission of the organization;

- to hire the technical experts to staff the office;

- to make sure those experts are working efficiently, effectively, and happily–so they can do their best work;

- to make sure they hit their deadlines. When obstacles arise, CEOs remove those obstacles.

That is what makes a great CEO–a team leader, a coach, and a problem solver.

Dark Moments

Why do things go wrong? There are a million possibilities but, often, it's because you overthink everything and talk yourself out of an opportunity by saying, "I can't put the people together," or "I can't coordinate this," or, in some other way, "I can't do this."

Then you get into that zone where you can't win, period, because you put yourself in such a corner where you're always thinking, "Nothing's going to work, so why bother?"

We've all done it, but when that becomes your default or go-to response, failure awaits.

We've all seen great things done by ordinary people. How do they do it? Remember the old joke, "How do you eat an elephant?" The simple yet brilliant answer? "One bite at a time."

Instead of saying, "I can't do all of this," try saying, "All I have to do is take these first two steps." From there, do two more, and two more, and, so on, until you've done them all.

I have tremendous respect for the US Navy SEALs. They were first organized during World War II and have operated under various names over the years, including Naval Combat Demolition Units (NCDUs) and Underwater Demolition Teams (UCTs). These sailors conducted dangerous operations that paved a path for success by their surface warfare brothers-in-arms. Recognizing the need to expand the role, some UDT personnel were given additional training and assigned to what is now called the Navy Sea, Air, and Land (SEAL) Teams, which continue to serve America in some of the riskiest situations imaginable. For most human beings, completing SEAL training isn't just an unrealistic goal; it is, literally, impossible.

I doubt that, in the prime of my life, I could last even a half day of that drill. The Navy recruits about 40,000 men and women each year. About half express interest in SEAL testing. Of those, only 1,000 actually apply–the rest, I think, get scared off–and 75 percent of them quit or are dropped. Altogether, just over one-half of one percent of each year's recruits actually become SEALs.

I mention them because SEAL training might be the most intense, most challenging, most gut-busting, spirit-breaking training in any military on Earth. To put it bluntly, those guys are nuts! Their whole training regimen is a dark moment where your physical, mental, and emotional strengths are tested to the limit of human endurance and beyond. Never mind how they'll complete their training, I want to know how they survived it! The answer is surprisingly simple.

When they enter SEAL training, their focus shifts entirely to the Trident—the nickname of the SEAL badge they'll wear throughout their naval careers, if they succeed. They commit to do whatever it takes to get that Trident. Their mindset becomes, "I'm gonna pin the Trident on my uniform, or they'll pin it on the coffin when they bury me."

I mentioned this at the beginning of the chapter:

> Shoot for the stars, you might land on the roof.
> Shoot for the roof, you might land in the trash can.
>
> —Modern Proverb

There is a third, rarely mentioned option:

> Shoot for the stars, and you might just reach them.

Those who've earned the Trident have reached the stars.

CHAPTER 4

Self Awareness of Your Problems

Gratitude

I repeat:

> Ability is what you're capable of doing. Motivation determines what you do. Attitude determines how well you do it. —Lou Holtz

> Discipline is a skill like any other, some naturally have more than others, but every single one of us can develop more. —Jocko Willink

The Basics

Gratitude is an attitude. (I know that sounds almost insultingly childish, but things like this should be so simple that every child can understand them.) It's similar to, and maybe we could say, a twin sibling of humility. Just as a humble person is aware that they don't know everything, a grateful person is aware that they didn't achieve everything solo. Knowing that others have helped us become what we are, shouldn't we be grateful? (Again, I know it's a simple question—almost childishly so—but so many people get it wrong.)

That said, what should we be grateful for?

That's not a childishly simple question—it involves some of life's most fundamental questions. And too often, we just need a reminder.

Do you feel gratitude for the simple act of breathing? Are you aware of—and truly thankful—for every single breath that fills your lungs? And who or what are you grateful to—God, the random universe, something else? It's a little cliché to say that we take these simple things for granted but cliches stick around for a reason: they keep being true!

Are you grateful for the basics of life? In America, that includes life, liberty, the pursuit of your version of happiness, the privilege of choosing your government—and when that government becomes obnoxious, the right to challenge it, and maybe even change it.

Are you grateful to be able to eat, drink, and sleep without having a tube down your throat? I'm serious—I was in a hospital not too long ago and saw a man sitting there with a tube in his side. I thought to myself, "You know what? I've never had it that bad!"

Be grateful—the fact that you're reading this book means there are millions of people across the globe who would love to be in your shoes.

Earlier, I mentioned my writing coach and hinted that he'd come up again. In 2018, he awoke with pain in his chest. He'd been feeling off for about ten days, but the symptoms didn't match the usual signs a heart attack, so he ignored them. But that day, he could not ignore them anymore, and emergency services arrived, his blood pressure was 203/130. (Later that day, his sister-in-law—a nurse—said, "Wow, I didn't know it could go that high." Yeah, not exactly the kind of thing you want to hear on a day like that.) Obviously, he survived—but in a very real way, he also died that day. His heart stopped twice:

once as he was being gurneyed into the hospital and, again while the ER team was assessing him.

Question: Do you think he looks at his daily life with more gratitude? Answer: Damn right he does.

By the way, he's very grateful for three more things:

Timing: As the paramedics were treating him, he said to the lead medic, "I almost waited a half hour before calling you." The paramedic didn't miss a beat, "Yeah, I think we'd be doing a recovery, not a rescue—and I don't think it would've worked."

Precision: Rescue and ER personnel require years of training and experience to save lives, and their licenses require ongoing training. His "cure" was scouring a load of cholesterol out of coach's coronary arteries and placing stents in those arteries. That means putting two incredibly tiny tudes of metal inside two incredibly tiny tudes of flesh!

Synchronicity: In the next chapter, I'll tell the story of when I heard a voice—and what happened as a result. But for now, let's go back to that near-fatal day. Later that evening, my coach lay in his hospital bed. This was during one of his "poor, starving artist" periods. He was unemployed, but a promising job opportunity was just around the corner. Despondent over the timing, he just looked up toward heaven and said, "Six more months and I'd have had cash in the bank, insurance, and everything else I needed to get through this. Why now?" A voice spoke clearly to his mind, answering simply, "To get it out of the way."

Take from that what you will. Believe we heard voices or not. Both of us are deeply grateful that the voice spoke when we needed to hear it.

Be Mission Driven

Do you believe that we are all born with a mission? I do, absolutely. Some people will cry or moan, "Why me?" I always respond, "Why not you?"

I am absolutely convinced that what I go through shapes me, frames me, and develops me into the individual that I need to be so I can make a difference in the world. A few of us will reshape the entire world, while the rest of us can reshape our small piece of it. I'm content with the small changes. I'm content being that guy designed for certain situations where I can help others. I've come to know that if I go through those trials and tribulations necessary, I'll become a man capable of fulfilling my mission.

I believe the same thing is true for everyone on Earth. Our missions differ, so the challenges differ, but we all have them.

I'm a religious person; I believe God predetermined our missions, our destiny. I don't think it's predetermined in the way of "this is how it will be, no matter what!" I'm more of the opinion that our mission is what Mr. Spock called our "first, best destiny." I like the phrasing. A lot of people, I think, want to refuse that destiny. They say to themselves, "No, no, no, no!"–and, as a result, they end up missing out, doing things that have nothing to do with what they should be doing, or what they most definitely *can* be doing.

Embrace the fact that if you stay focused and true to your purpose, God (or fate, or the universe, or whatever you believe in) will get you to where you need to be. You'll pass through trials and tribulations, but you'll grow stronger, more skilled, more determined–and ultimately, you'll be a better person. That's all part of your destiny.

It's akin to being hardened like a piece of steel, which is heated until it glows and is then plunged into cold water or oil. Hardening makes steel stronger—it'll strengthen you until you're equal to your mission. A couple of additional biblical verses to encourage you:

- *"Behold, I have refined thee, but not with silver; I have chosen thee in the furnace of affliction"* (Isaiah 48:10, KJV).

- *"To every thing there is a season, and a time to every purpose under the heaven"* (Ecclesiastes 3:1, KJV).

I'm going to top it off by saying this: when the Bible talks about seasons, it's important to remember that some people are designed to be on this planet for only a brief season. I used to wonder why there are babies who die so young. Maybe that person was sent there for a particular purpose, and it just didn't take them long to complete that purpose. Maybe they just had to bring a certain level of joy, provide certain experiences to us, and create a certain connection to somebody—and then, they were called home. I don't know. Some people are here for a certain season, and then that season is done. Take from that short season what you can—I'm betting it's more than you'd imagine it could be.

For the rest of us, the Preacher offers several examples, including "a time to sow, a time to reap."

I remind you, recognizing the right time or season is vital.

Discerning Your Mission

Now, we get into an interesting discussion: short of a revelation from God, how do you find your mission in life? I think the real question is, "Are you listening?"

There's a voice—from God, fate, or the universe—that you can hear if you're listening.

Sometimes, it's a real voice. Years ago, I was walking down the street with a lady I was. We were about to cross the street when I heard a voice saying, "Knock her down!" Almost without thinking, I pushed her into the bushes. At that moment, a pizza delivery guy came flying down the street. He would've killed her. He stopped when he realized what had happened.

Not fully realizing the situation, she was not happy, "Why did you push me?"

I said, "If I hadn't, you'd have been dead. Something just told me to push you in the bushes." I didn't know what it was then, and I still don't today, but it was something real.

We also have experiences where we don't hear that voice because we aren't listening. Those generally don't go well.

In general terms, we often don't recognize what we're good at because we're not focused on the signs that are guiding us in the right direction. To add to my earlier point: *if you can look at the person in the mirror and say, "I'm not doing the best work I can do, and I need to figure out what my best work is," then you're halfway home.*

CHAPTER 5

Inherited Problems and Family Curses

We all carry things from our family and our environment. When these issues pass through several generations, they become what's often referred to as "the family curse."

That's a cover-up—there's no such thing as a curse. These are bad practices based on incorrect ideas about life and child-rearing. They get passed from generation to generation because people assume they can't be changed. But they can. We simply need to recognize them for what they are and decide not to continue the *status quo*.

My family's "curse" was what I'd call generational bickering between father and son. Like a pride of lions, fathers fought with their sons over who would be the "alpha" in the family. For example, my father left home when I was in my early 20s because he'd lost my mother's respect and, in his mind, was no longer the alpha. That was a bad decision—he walked away from the problem instead of facing and fixing it, and my family suffered as a result. (More on this to follow.)

Eventually, I figured this whole "curse" thing out, and now I'm doing my best to stop it from continuing into my children's generation.

Baggage from the Past

Having a positive relationship with our past and personal background is vital to advancing along our path to a better, brighter future. Studies have shown that memories are not immutable but contain distortions and creations of their own. In other words, our brains are not computers—they aren't audio or video recorders capturing all that we have experienced in precise detail. The past leaves an imprint on us, but we do not remember the exact details—we are more attuned to the emotions we felt.

In fact, the common thread in most of our memories is not the facts themselves, but the meaning we attach to them. For example, two people were abandoned by their parents at a very young age. Both suffered greatly, but one embarked on a process of understanding how and why this happened. A few years later, this person remembers the event as a sad memory, but with an understanding of the circumstances surrounding it. The other person, who has not "digested" the experience, only has vague and inaccurate memories, along with a strong sense of pain and resentment.

It's never a question of what we've experienced but how we've chosen to deal with it. Many of the reasons you feel anxious or sad are rooted in past events that you haven't fully processed. These unresolved issues continue to be a negative factor in your life.

Past Experiences and Their Interpretation

Memory plays a significant role in our lives. The past is actually a complex concept because, in spite of the fact that it is over, it can continually influence the present—even if we don't notice it.

I'll refer you to the classic building metaphor: First, the foundations are built, and then each floor is built on top of the one before it. If the foundations are not properly constructed, the upper floors may begin to crack or shift for no apparent reason. In the event of an earthquake or some other major disturbance, the whole building could collapse.

The same happens to people. We build the foundations of what we are in the first years of life, but most of our earliest childhood memories reside only in our subconscious. As our awareness of the world increases, each experience adds up and is interpreted through the lens of unrecalled memories. If that foundation is compromised, for any reason, it is possible that our life can crack or become unstable, putting everything at risk. Even decades later, memories can resurface or affect us, lingering in our subconscious despite remaining hidden.

Although the building metaphor is useful in creating a basic understanding of our psyches, the human being is much more complex and flexible. Understanding allows us to interpret what happened in the past in a more constructive and useful way. That is to say, what we have experienced helps us improve or make us worse, depending on how we interpret it.

Past Experiences Can Be Reinterpreted

As a self-defense mechanism, we tend to forget negative experiences such as abandonment, rejection, or any form of physical, mental, or emotional trauma. We bury these memories deep in our subconscious, never thinking about them. We do this to avoid immersing ourselves in thoughts that do not contribute to our emotional wellbeing.

However, when we do not give ourselves the time to assimilate and process those experiences, we keep the experience alive in our subconscious. This results in sorrow or anxiety—feelings that seem to have no explanation. What we have lived doesn't matter as much as how we've defined the memory of it. If we choose a victim-oriented interpretation of the facts, we'll see our past through the lens of self-pity. If we choose a defensive orientation, we'll have reason to be wary of others or adopt an attitude of vendetta—the need for revenge on others—even if they really didn't do anything to harm us.

It's important to learn how to dismantle our experiences. This means taking a step back and adopting the perspective that helps us understand their true significance. For example, a smaller-than-average child will likely be bullied. This can lead to feelings of self-pity (the "nobody loves me" syndrome) or paranoia (the "everybody's out to get me" syndrome). Neither of these is true. That child's experience has no significance to their adult life. It was simply the unfortunate, and all too common, result of the childish arrogance of bigger children.

Perhaps that bullying child did not act from personal malice. Perhaps they were also a victim of abuse. Children repeat the example of parents. Perhaps there are undiscovered mental health issues that cause the misbehavior. Regardless of another person's motivation, the best way to handle injustice is to recognize that the world will never be perfectly just. Instead, see yourself as someone who has successfully lived through a negative episode, overcome it, and found happiness.

Control Your Mind

Acknowledging

You can't fix a problem unless you know there is a problem.

Obviously, right? Only then can you begin to create a course of action to fix it. We've all heard the statement, "Insanity is repeating the same actions and expecting a different result." Take, for example, a family with a history of substance abuse. If you realize this problem persists, it might be because no one is actually stopping to ask, "Why is every family member struggling with addiction?" There's something going on here that nobody's addressing, and sometimes, just asking the right the question is part of the solution. For example:

Question: Why is everybody in this family an addict?

Answer: Because everybody in this family is an addict.

When new members enter the family—via marriage or birth—they enter a world where addiction is the norm. We all want to be seen as "normal" and feel accepted by those important to us, so we tend to do what "everybody" is doing. Even if we know they're doing wrong, we can easily fall into a trap of needing to fit in.

How do we break this cycle? First, we must realize that it's happening. Sometimes, that's not very hard but other times, the problems are so subtle that they can easily fly under people's radar.

Then, we must ask those hard questions and take those hard answers seriously.

By the way, there are always signs, but most of us aren't well-equipped to see them. I've spoken with many public school teachers who say they can always tell which kids are likely to end up as criminals. So, I ask: if the teachers can see this, why are we not directing resources to address these problems while those problems are still in their early stages? If we can see it early on, how can we steer these children away from becoming a danger to themselves and others? I, for one, wish I knew.

Fixing

We've done it with some problems. Back in the 1960s, bullying was a huge problem in public schools. The attitude of school counselors, teachers, administrators—even parents—was something like, "Well, boys will be boys." (And, we didn't even acknowledge that girls did it too!) We let it happen because society at the time assumed it couldn't change.

It hasn't changed enough—bullying is still a problem, but today, we're fighting back. As a society, we have engaged the challenge. Individuals and families can do the same on a smaller scale.

For example, someone might say, "Oh, mom is co-dependent—that's why she acts the way she does." Then they wonder, "Am I co-dependent? Am I acting that way with my children?" Nobody wants to have that conversation, and that is why the family is "cursed."

I have a friend who's been in a situation where the volatility in their family has been going on for years. She shared that one of her relatives has completely cut ties with the family and has no contact with the others.

"How is that one doing?" I asked.

"Doing well," was her reply.

"Well, then, don't you think it's time for you to do the same?" Because they all stayed around each other—fighting all the time—their whole family dynamic became toxic. One family member left and hasn't returned, now living a better life, while my friend remains stuck in that verbally violent environment.

Nobody just "gets" ahead, you have to "take" ahead, if you get my meaning.

On hearing this story, another friend said, "Yeah, I had a lot of that in my family. We seem to get along a lot better with some distance between us." **That** is thinking out of the box. Most families assume that proximity is a plus. For most families, it is, but not for all.

I'd like to give you a clear, all-inclusive list of ways to fix family curses, but no such list exists. Each problem is as unique as the individuals involved.

Here are the keys I can offer:

- Forget shortcuts and easy answers.

- Think outside the box.

- However hard it is, push through until it is **done**.

- Expect a painful recovery.

CHAPTER 6

Accepting then Re-Programming

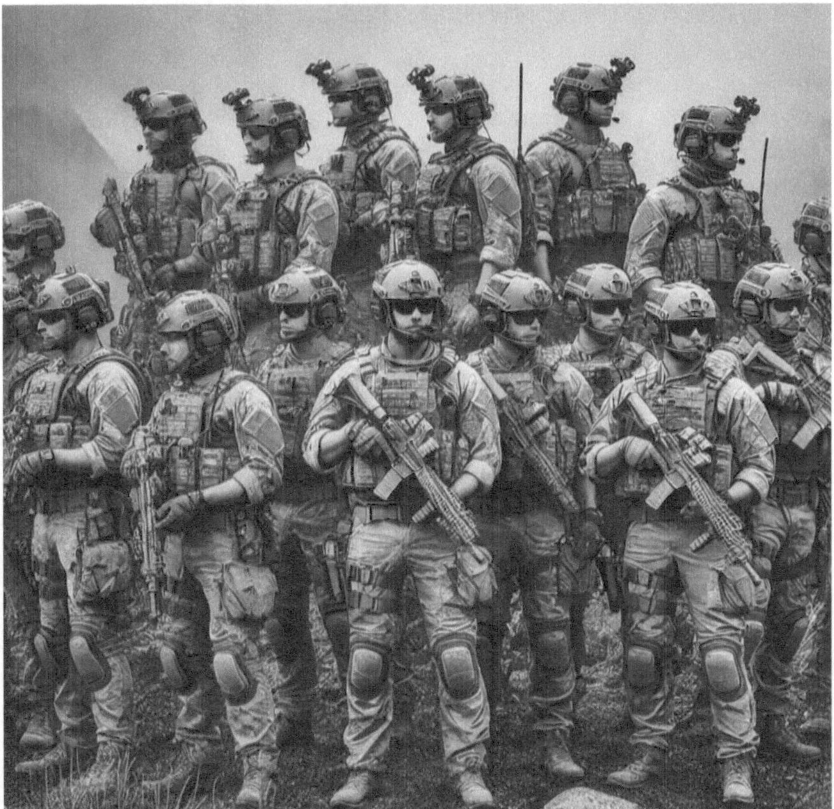

Accepting My Current Life

Imagine waking up every morning feeling empty and sad. Why do you feel that way?

Perhaps because you see yourself following the same routine, doing everything on autopilot, day after day: breakfast, coffee, shower, commute, work, lunch, work, gym, shopping, dinner, drinks, video, bed. Imagine having the same conversations with yourself every day: "I feel like I'm existing, not *living*! I feel no joy, just the monotony of predictable days." That's grim.

There's nothing worse than feeling like you have no control over your life or an idea how to make it better. If you feel that way but don't feel confused or embittered, you are one in a million.

What's the root of this? Well, there are probably as many answers to that question as there are people asking it. Let me deal with one: so many people focus on what they don't have and therefore, they're dissatisfied or distressed–some even fall into deep depression. In some cases, depression is understandable. They may lack good health, struggle to earn a living, or find themselves in difficult family situations. These are real problems.

However, most people who are distressed or depressed about what they don't have are those who view life as if it's set in stone, as if the rule is, "This is it, it can't change."

This isn't it.

There are things in life we can't change. It's been said that each of us has some kind of disability, though I'm not sure if that's an absolute truth. But what I do know is that we all, absolutely, face challenges. We all face loss, tough times, and more. I wrote this book to show people that bad times are normal but fixable. Some disabilities, of course, can't be undone, but we can fix our outlook on life. We can still prosper, no matter what the universe throws at us.

Get Ready to Move Forward

As I've mentioned in the previous chapter, you can't fix a problem unless you know there is a problem.

I don't feel debilitating emotions because I feel deep gratitude for what I have. That said, I'm never entirely satisfied with my life. I question myself:

- Do I feel like I'm missing something? And why do I miss it?

- Am I missing my mark—my destiny, my fullest happiness?

- How far have I *really* come in life?

- If I have everything else going for me—good job, good family, good friends—why does it still feel like I am missing what truly matters right now?

- How did I miss that mark?

These are hard questions, and they might generate hard answers. Hard answers are good—they mean you're being serious about this personal progress interview. Let's look at a simple example of not getting what we want:

How'd I miss getting the better car I need? Well, suppose that a bank sent me a pre-approved application for a car loan. (And I mean a *real* bank—like Chase or Wells Fargo. Not the "Last Weirdness Bank of Podunk, Iowa." FYI, there are *two* real towns named Podunk, but neither one is in Iowa. So don't be fooled!)

Well, I tore it up, thinking it might be a scam. It wasn't—it was legit. I could've done my due diligence, verified it, and driven off with a better car I actually needed But no. At that time, I had $10,000 sitting in the bank… and I used it to buy a snowmobile. I chose badly.

We've all chosen badly at times, and we are where we are based on all our choices—good and bad. So, now what?

We choose differently.

1. Start with Your Values

Values are, obviously, what we hold as important—literally, what we value. They're the basis of every choice we make. They guide our emotions and influence our level of satisfaction. They are the standard by which we judge our life and our happiness.

Healthy values do not change over time—they lead us to be better people and to perform positive actions that do not harm someone else's happiness. Unhealthy values, on the other hand, may change overnight to suit the situation, which causes uncertainties, which might lead us to improper acts, which lead us to degrade ourselves and others.

Determining Your Values

That personal progress interview mentioned earlier can be a great way to sit down with yourself (and your spouse, if applicable) and take a real look at your values. (That means asking yourself more hard questions, if you haven't guessed that already.) Questions like:

- What matters so much to me that I know will still be important in twenty, thirty, even forty years down the road?

- What do I hold so dear that I will defend it with my life?

- What do I want people to remember me for? What will my legacy be?

- If I died today, what would people write on my tombstone?

And, the ultimate self-examination questions:

- In the eternal scheme of things: Who am I? Why am I here?

I can't tell you what your values are. I won't try to tell you what they should be. That's entirely on you. I will give you one piece of advice: As you're doing all this self-analysis, don't leave God out of the equation.

This level of self-analysis? It's tough—even for the most self-aware among us. So, if you're new to this and need a way to jumpstart the process, I suggest a review of your past actions to help you begin to understand who you are. Dig deep and ask yourself, "Why did I make those choices?" Why did I choose university over trade school? Why did I getting married young or wait? Why did I decide to have children immediately—or not at all? Each of these possibilities contains a choice made, based on a precise value.

Take it a step further. In some circles, there's a principle called "The Five Whys." This principle suggests that it might take five questions to reach the real reason for an action. For example:

Why did you go to university?

To get an education and develop saleable skills.

Why develop saleable skills?

To make better money.

Why do you need to make better money?

> *To increase my family's financial security.*

Why do you worry about financial security?

> *Because my parents never had any.*

Why did your parents not have security?

> *Because they never got a proper education.*

Aha! Now we have true motivation. Let's say this person' included some financial insecurity, possibly leading to missed opportunities and almost certainly causing envy toward those who had more. As a newly-minted adult, this person makes choices designed to avoid the missed opportunities that plagued their childhood. That's a good value based on experience. What was their experience? Our culture says a college education is the gateway to prosperity. My parents didn't obtain degrees and didn't achieve prosperity. Therefore, I need the degree to cross through that gateway into prosperity.

On one hand, the logic is flawed—many have achieved prosperity without collegiate education. Among the trades, many men and women make very good livings—sometimes out-earning professionals and without crushing student debt.

On the other hand, such a childhood can cause one to take it too far. Instead of "financially secure" as a goal, one might lose a little of their sanity and adopt a 1980s bumper sticker as their fiscal mantra, "Who dies with the most toys wins." Moderation, rationality, intelligent thought—in short, maturity—should always govern our choice of values.

2. Choose Healthy Situations

Having gone through this serious self-analysis, you should be determined to avoid situations where you're tempted to cross the line. You should feel empowered to create situations that reflect your true self. Situational awareness and determined effort save us from unhappiness—the negative consequences of bad decisions. Staying on your chosen path (a straight and narrow one, I hope), allows you to quickly find the right antidote to doubts and problems.

3. The "Oops" Moment

Speaking of problems, there may come a time in your life when everything stops and you say, "Oops!"

A time when you've remained firm in your values and, yet it didn't work out as you hoped or planned. You realize that you've reached the end of the book of rules—metaphorically speaking—that you wrote for yourself. The rules, which naturally followed from your values, didn't get you where you wanted to be.

Time for another question: How far have you really come in life?

That's about as esoteric a question as you'll ever meet because it's related to another question which many people never think to ask: How far can I go in life?

That question really comes to the surface in "oops" moments. Theoretically speaking, the interesting part about seeing how far you've already come—the education you've completed, the credentials you've earned, the marriage, the kids, the awards, the respect of family, friends, and coworkers—should show you that you've come further than most people.

But, how far have you really come compared to how far you could go? Are you where you *should* be compared to where you *could* be? Have you missed the mark—the critical moments where you could've done more or do better than you did?

Think about it this way: everybody's walking around, patting you on the back, showering you with compliments—maybe even making you a little embarrassed by the attention—but, at the same time, you're beginning to feel discontented thinking those accomplishments are your only life legacy.

Congratulations, you are officially suffering a mid-life crisis!

You, despite your best efforts, have not achieved your American Dream. You're still stuck in limbo, thinking, "Alright, I did all these things because this was what was expected of me. Even so, here I am, dissatisfied with the life I created."

4. Get Up and Go

Just as you did with that first personal progress interview, you have examined yourself and determined your present place in life. You still feel the need to make a significant change.

Good. Do it!

Don't wait for "the right time." Don't expect a sign from heaven (but be very grateful if one does appear). Don't think the world can answer these questions or solve this riddle for you. You need to get up, do the work, make the decisions, and reap, on your own, the success or failure of that decision.

A lot of people fail when they get to this point.

They fall short because they're not willing to put in the effort required to make truly significant changes in life. Why not? They don't see the viability of this work. They don't see it making difference. I'm going to venture a guess: That atti-tude means they don't know whether or not they have time or resources to put that much effort into something new because they don't know if the reward is going to be there.

At mid-life, most people start thinking about remuneration. If I put in this effort, what's the payoff going to be?

I wish I could tell you. You alone get to decide what the payoff might be, and you alone get to decide if that potential payoff is worth the resources you'll expend to reach whatever goal you're contemplating.

Remember the original premise: timing, precision, and synchronicity are the determining factors of success. If you can recognize the opportunity of the moment and seize it; if you have the precision to do the work right; if you're the kind of person who attracts the right people, you'll develop the synchronicity you need to blend your skillset with theirs into a winning combination.

This may involve sailing into unknown waters where many sailors have been shipwrecked before. Don't let that dissuade you. Go forward with faith in yourself, your values, and your plan. Be daring but not reckless—because if you are reckless, you will (almost certainly) not end up wreck less! Practice proactive situational awareness and deter-mined effort.

5. Review and Revise

Progress interviews aren't for people alone. At regular inter-vals, depending on your particular program, you need to pause (while everyone else keeps working) to assess what's working and make adjustments to what isn't.

20 Questions to Assist You Along the Way

Instead of laying out a list of steps—because no two paths are the same—I'm falling back on something I've done before: ask you a series of questions. Some will be harder than others, but all are geared to focus your mind on the future and what it could hold. No matter where you are in life or what you're currently doing, some questions might not apply to you, but most will help you look within and guide you toward a new direction.

1. What would you do if you're told that you only have ten more years to live?

Narrowing the time span of existence helps give some perspective.

Look at the next ten years. It's enough to allow us to see the end of it all, while giving importance to every year, every month, and every day. Now, ask yourself what choices will you make for that last decade?

2. What are you afraid of?

Fears are like fences that limit our freedom.

If you want to fully understand who you are, ask yourself: what fears have influenced your life the most? Imagine who you could be without those fears holding you back.

3. What are your best and worst features?

Sit down during one of those personal progress interviews and make a list of your strengths, then another list for your weaknesses. Ask yourself how you can take advantage of the strengths and improve the weaknesses.

Congratulations, you have a new hobby. Some people renovate houses or rehabilitate cars—you can renovate yourself!

4. Do you often feel sad for no reason?

Our moods are the most useful indicators of whether we're living in alignment with what's right or wrong for us.

Some of us deal with mental health issues—things beyond their control. For the rest of us, moods give us information about our inner self and the effectiveness of our lifestyle. Negative emotions, such as sorrow or depression, can be a message that something needs to change within us. That change might relate to a perspective, a circumstance, or a relationship.

5. How does three days of solitude affect you?

The ability to feel good about yourself also means feeling good alone. On the other hand, not feeling good about being alone could mean that you don't know yourself so well that you really like your own company. (If you don't, no one else will.) Maybe spending some time alone—at home, on a vacation, or a retreat of some kind—will allow you to learn new things about yourself that you'll end up liking—and, just maybe, a few things that you would need to change, too.

6. How have you changed since you were little?

The past is a valuable source of information about who we were, who we are, and who we could be. Reflect on the child you once were: What was important to you, what was fun, what inspired you, what scared you? Answering these questions honestly can reveal a lot about you.

7. How do you feel when you think back to your past?

It's not possible to be objective about ourselves. It's equally impossible to remember every single moment you've experienced. An old sage once said, "History is a collective guess based on an incomplete record which was usually written by the winners and always written with a bias."

When you think back on the past, try not to lend too much weight to one side or the other, and most definitely, don't focus too much on the bad memories. We all have them, but with extremely rare exceptions, they are the minority of our experiences.

There are moments of beauty in every life. Learn to recognize and remember them. They will help keep your outlook positive.

8. What's important to you in a partner?

Some encourage us with, "Opposites attract," while others champion, "Marry your twin." The true path generally lies between those extremes. This is true of marital, business, and every other type of partnership you'll encounter.

What should you look for in a partner? One should start by knowing one's own strengths and weaknesses. (There I go again, encouraging self-examination. It's often not fun, but I promise you this is vital knowledge for success.) Choose a partner who can support your weaknesses with their strengths, and vice versa. You might say, marry your mirror image or, at least, someone who mirrors a part of you. Synergy, in a marriage or partnership of any kind, is where miracles happen.

9. How do you see yourself in ten years?

I've suggested keeping your focus on the long-term. Thinking about what people will say at your funeral is a mental trick that helps you focus on what you want to accomplish in life.

What do you see yourself doing? How do you see yourself acting? What are you hoping for? Answer these questions for the ten years, then break that goal down into five-year, two-year, and one-year benchmarks. Suddenly, it's not so hard to imagine.

10. Apart from time and money, what do you want from life?

Everybody (except for those who already have enough) wants more money. Money is a tool that gets you other things you want. Everybody (except for those who already have too much on their hands) wants more time to spend as they choose, rather than as others dictate. I think these facts might be common to virtually every human being in the world.

Therefore, ignore them as core goals. Think about what you'd want from life if time and money weren't an issue—if you already had enough of both.

That's where your true essence resides.

11. What makes you happy?

Think back to the most beautiful and happy moments of your life. What do they have in common?

When did you feel perfectly at peace with yourself and with the universe?

Challenge: How can you create more moments like those?

12. How could you help others?

What talents or skills or personality traits do you have, or might you develop, that could add value to the lives of others?

They do not necessarily have to be skills that can be employed in the marketplace. The ability to listen without judgment and without comment is priceless. It could reveal an aptitude for a mental health profession or in counseling. Equally, if not more so, it could make you the friend people need during the worst times of their lives.

Don't underestimate even the smallest of your strengths.

13. What catches your interest on a daily basis?

What do you like to talk about? When do you feel your attention riveted? What activities make you feel enthusiastic and fully engaged?

Do more of them. Invite your friends with similar interests. Make it a party.

14. What is your idea of success?

This is another question that serves to identify your center—your guiding values.

How do you define "success" for yourself? A strong family? A home? Good health? Professional achievement? Community involvement? Public service? Private service?

An old sage once said, "There are as many definitions of profit as there are enterprises to engage." Another wise person said, "If you don't know where you're going, you'll probably end up somewhere else."

Listen to them.

15. Who do you admire?

Who are your points of reference?

What characteristics do they possess that you want to emulate?

Decide to develop those characteristics.

16. What are you missing from life, and how could you get it?

Fullness in life is achieved through a mix of material, spiritual, and cognitive things.

In which area of life are you dissatisfied? Relationships? Work? Friendships? Fun?

Analyze your dissatisfactions by limiting them to specific areas. That is, don't get caught up in the idea that everything is negative.

Identify one deficiency at a time. Then ask yourself what you could do to fix it.

Then fix it and move on to another.

17. What is essential for you? What could you not do without?

What are the cornerstones in the foundation of your life? The people, the work, the activities, the interests?

Riddle me this: If your house was on fire and you had time to grab just three or four things, which things would you save?

18. If you had to describe yourself by just two or three qualities, which would you choose?

What defines you most?

Is that definition accurate and complete?

Is that the definition you want?

19. Do you ever dream of running away and changing your life?

I mean, do you ever feel stuck in a life that doesn't seem to belong to you?

If you got the green light tomorrow, if you suddenly had the means to go wherever you want to go and do whatever you want to do without consequences, what would you do?

20. Do you respect and trust yourself?

This is crucial—the most important question. After all this talk about values and interests—of what we are and what we are not—in the final analysis, it's all worthless unless we love and trust ourselves.

We are—with very few exceptions—wonderful people. We're flawed but we're trying and, in spite of those flaws, we're able to achieve some wonderful things. We should never judge ourselves based on our worst moments or biggest failures, but rather as children—still learning, still growing—with infinite potential.

If we can't learn to love ourselves, we'll never care enough to discover what wonderful people the rest of humanity is.

Trust yourself. Respect yourself. You've earned it.

And, if not, repentance is still part of the gospel.

CHAPTER 7

Effective Change–The Mindset of Progress

"Change" is a neutral term. I'm not about change for the sake of change; I'm about **effective change**.

When looking at change, anyone can change something at any time, but is that change effective? You may be doing something new, but are you doing something that will actually bring about a future that doesn't include the patterns of the past?

For example, my writing coach missed his opportunity in Hollywood, but he's now making a good living helping folks like me, and he's using my TPS strategy:

Timing

His plan for retirement? Doesn't have one. Although he recently reached the traditional retirement age, he plans to continue working as long as he's able to. Partly, that's because his original dream didn't work out for him but equally because he loves what he's doing. His time is his own, and he uses part of it (he calls himself "semi-retired") to help people like me.

Precision

He spent many years learning his profession: As a copywriter, he has written over half a million words for a major retailer. As a journalist, he has written numerous articles for local, regional, and national newspapers and magazines. As a corporate communicator, people have asked him a lot of questions and he has become particularly good at finding answers. Combined with the storytelling skills he learned in his film degree, he's developed a precise and successful style for this kind of writing, and he's now developing new skills as an interviewer in his present role.

Synchronization

He came to this new career through a friend, who suggested it at a time when coach was looking for a new opportunity because his business was slumping. That friend connected him with people who could make the new plan work. He synchronized his efforts with the work of others who had expertise he lacked. Together, they are a formidable team.

What are the obstacles?

To make effective changes, you must make and implement a declaration then stick to it, never crossing that line again. You have to be forceful and consistent about doing things differently.

You

The Bible says, "The spirit indeed is willing, but the flesh is weak." Too true. We're all adults, we know what's right. But we're all human—we struggle to do it. It's normal. It might be the basic struggle of humanity—this idea of consistently doing what's right. You have to push through the drudgery of learning if change is to be effective. That willingness to push through is nothing more than an attitude towards your own success. Successful people are willing to do what unsuccessful people are unwilling to do: whatever is necessary to succeed.

For example, if you want to renovate a house, what's the first thing you do? You tear it down!

Change frequently starts with making a mess. Effective change means identifying the old parts of you that aren't working and ripping them out of your life. It's like a house: the paint is peeling, so you strip it off. The roof is leaking, so the drywall has gotten wet. So, you rip off and replace them both. The old must go to make room for the new. Anyone, when it comes to renovating a house, can see the need for demolition. When it comes to renovating ourselves–losing all that emotional baggage or those bad attitudes–most of us say, "No, oh, no, I can't do that!" And that's true, if you can't conceive it, you can't make it happen.

By the way, that's a personal problem that can become a public problem. People who refuse to effectively change their own lives (their lack of success) tend to project their problems onto others. Your attitude toward someone else's success can also be a problem. As a shop manager, for example, you need to want others to succeed–even to the point that their success exceeds yours. You must respect people, their skills, their common sense, and other attributes. You can't micromanage, degrade, make fun of, or, in any way treat people with less respect than the respect you want for yourself. So, stop it. People should not have to walk on eggshells around you.

Also You

Some changes require new skills. For example, when you enter a life or business partnership, you have new obligations that never existed before. Your partner has the right to know what you're doing, where you are, and so on. Your old communication skills may not be up to these new relationships. You have to deal with partners in ways that differ from other relationships. When you become a parent, you have to deal with your children differently than the way you deal with other people. These are new skills you must develop.

Similarly, when you undertake a new physical fitness program or a new job, you may need new technical skills. Mountaineering, bodybuilding, cycling, marathoning, and other pursuits have rules if you want to be effective. Success depends on following those rules, just like changing jobs from an auto mechanic to an insurance salesman or a plumber to a woodworker. Fail to acquire those new skills, and you will fail to achieve effective change.

Totally You

In the last chapter, I wrote about failure. Something inside you is not working or you did the best you could and still fell short of your dreams.

What's next?

You now have to look for a new dream—your old dream has to be revamped or discarded. You might have to, as a friend likes to say, "Chug a mug of reality." Let's say there are ten levels of success, ranging from "survival" to "mega-stardom." You've realized that you aren't destined for tenth-level success, so, you go for seventh-level success.

You have, theoretically, realigned with the realistic. (You might still be wrong—you might top out at fifth- or sixth-level, but let's be optimistic!) Can you realign? Can you be realistic? Can you focus on the new agenda?

Once I've decided to pursue something new, I've established a new realm of activity for myself. My new agenda must include three elements: Realignment, reality, and realm. That's my new dream and agenda.

Your Limits are Undefined

Think about this: if you've ever watched little kids on the playground, you'll see that they have no idea of what they can and can't do. They'll just run up to things and look at them. They'll just jump in and do things. They'll climb a hill just three feet tall and act like they've reached Mount Everest's summit.

Now, look at yourself: if you take away your preconditions, your negative thoughts, your talent for confining yourself to a metaphorical straight jacket, you, too, can be childlike in a very positive way. You'll need endurance, stamina, willpower, and resistance—but you can rip up the whole concept of limitations in life. All things being equal, human nature tends towards doing remarkable things. But once you get involved into people's preconceived notions—their ideas, their thoughts—everything positive and powerful can be lost.

Having said that, there are those who would have us believe, "If you can conceive it, you can achieve it." **False!** You'll notice a similar statement, from the negative perspective, a few paragraphs ago. You might think these statements are exact opposites. **Also false!** Many of us dream about being rich and famous. Well, the guy who said, "There's plenty of room at the top," had a lot to learn about pyramids.

Reality means we sometimes set goals that are unachievable. As much as we want to make things happen, we don't always have the talent or skills to reach the level we dream about. Or, as I've noted before, what we dream might not be our destiny. God (the universe, fate, karma—whatever you believe in) may have other plans for us.

That, however, is only half the equation. How do you know you don't have the talent, skill, or resources? You try it! Your limits are undefinable because you don't know what they are until you've reached them, and that's generally a longer trip than that we give ourselves credit for. But you'll never know if you just sit at home fearing that you won't succeed. Take control of your life like you'd take control of a football, basketball, or soccer ball. Move forward with your best efforts until you've reached the end of your resources. Then, call friends and family—even strangers—if you need to. Avoid the temptation of outlandish goals, and there's nothing that can stop you from succeeding.

Determination and Endurance

CEOs and Cockroaches

Success doesn't take brilliance; achievement isn't just for prodigies. Look at the roach. Roaches have been around for about a billion years. What makes them consistently continue as a viable species with all the poisons and traps we set up to kill them?

Adaptability and resilience. You cannot kill them all. No matter where you are in this world, there's a roach still crawling around. Now, can we legitimately ascribe something so obscure as "determination" to a roach's intelligence? There's no way to know what's going on in their miniscule ant brains. Even so, we know that they've adapted, become resistant to multiple poisons, to different circumstances and climates, and to man's intrusion. They just keep going.

Let's look at the example of a CEO. They don't have to be the smartest people in the room; they need to get the right people in the room—people who can make the right decisions, people who can be, collectively, the equivalent of smartest person in the room.

Great CEOs don't need to know the answers to all the questions—they don't even need to know all the questions. They just need to surround themselves with the right talent, or, if they don't have it, they need to hire it—and they can turn around any failing company or take a good company and make it into a great one. The question then arises: Are you, Mr. or Madam CEO, determined to find that talent?

In that same vein, are you prepared to go to the distance? Are you really prepared to stick it out long enough to knock on a thousand doors and get to 1,001st door when somebody again says, "No"?

Are you the person that knocks on one more door and finally hears, "Hey, I'm interested in your product"?

In many cases, it's just a numbers game. There's a famous quote about Thomas Edison and the electric light bulb. In fact, it was a new battery that Edison and his people were working on:

> I found him at a bench about three feet wide and twelve to fifteen feet long, on which there were hundreds of little test cells that had been made up by his corps of chemists and experimenters. He was seated at this bench testing, figuring, and planning. I then learned that he had thus made over nine thousand experiments in trying to devise this new type of storage battery, but had not produced a single thing that promised to solve the question. In view of this immense amount of thought and labor, my sympathy got the better of my judgment, and I said: "Isn't it a shame that with the tremendous amount of work you have done you haven't been able to get any results?"
>
> Edison turned on me like a flash, and with a smile replied: "Results! Why, man, I have gotten a lot of results! I know several thousand things that won't work."
>
> —Walter S. Mallory[6]

Edison is regarded as the greatest inventor of America's Industrial Age. He should also be enshrined in a hall of fame for sheer willpower.

---

[6] Dyer, Frank Lewis and Thomas Commerford Martin. *Edison: His Life and Inventions*. New York: Harpers (now HarperCollins), 1910.

In the movie *Chariots of Fire*—a somewhat fictionalized account of Eric Liddell in the 1924 Olympic Games—Liddell intended to compete in the 100-yard dash. Finding that preliminary heats would take place on a Sunday, the devoutly religious Liddell refused to compete. He was, fortunately, able to run and win the gold medal in another event but as he sat with his trainer in the stands for the 100-yard finals—watching his chief rival take the gold—his trainer leaned over and asked, "Any regrets?"

Liddell smiled and quietly replied, "Aye, but no doubts."[7]

I don't think we get discouraged when our heart, gut, or whatever that inner voice is keeps saying, "No doubts." If it does, perhaps you're facing an illusion instead of the reality of where you should be versus where you are. This is often called "finding your niche in life."

It Begs the Question

How do I find my niche?

That is a very wise question. If I were to interview someone on this, I would begin by asking:

- Did you go to college out of necessity or choice?

- Did you go to college because your parents told you to?

- Did you go to college because society said that you need to have a college degree?

- Did you see something that you deeply wanted to do, and that credential was required to be accepted into that occupational community?

---

[7] Hudson, Hugh, director. *Chariots of Fire*. Allied Stars Ltd. and Enigma Productions, 1981.

Maybe you were very good at coaching. Does coaching require a bachelor's degree, or can you start with a trade school certificate and go out and coach yoga classes or be a physical fitness trainer? You can get a bachelor's in exercise physiology or another, similar discipline, but you don't need one to start or to be successful. If you were good at coaching and saw a good living in it but were so focused on the false idea that "I need to be an engineer" (for whatever external reason you feel impels you to study engineering), you'll never discover your coaching destiny. It's a question of following the advice of others or following your gut.

Cast a wide net. Do a lot of things. Experiment. Have several summer jobs during high school. However, you do it, find something you do well and love doing. Set a goal, "I will not go through life dreading the idea of going to work." (Don't laugh, that happens more often than any of us like to admit.)

Conquer your Environment

You are—in the final analysis—the only obstacle to your dreams. If you've chosen them wisely, you are the master or mistress of your fate. However, you are not alone on planet Earth, you have to deal with:

Them

What about others? Have you heard about the men and women who did their jobs well but still lost them when their company was bought out, merged, or had to downsize for some other reason? Of course, you have. Have you heard about the family that lost a parent to cancer, a car accident, or some other unforeseen circumstance? Of course, you have.

I won't say those have nothing to do with your plans. You wouldn't believe me—nor would I—if I said those weren't obstacles. They are. But they are not obstacles unique to you—someone is facing them every day. Some of those people adapted, innovated, and overcame. Yes, plans have to change in cases like those, but I return to my original premise—attitude, first and foremost.

The dream might have to change when new circumstances arise but with the right attitude, you can probably make some part of your dream work. If you had not noticed, those are people we celebrate: we give them awards, write books and make movies about their lives, flock to them by the thousands to hear and be motivated by their stories.

In a very different example, those of my generation will remember the Tylenol murders. Few actively remember how the company rebounded a regained its market share:

"Tylenol" is a brand name for acetaminophen, a popular non-aspirin pain reliever. In 1982, seven people in and around Chicago died because a still-unknown person laced Tylenol with cyanide. The manufacturer, Johnson & Johnson (J&J), immediately pulled out 31 million bottles of capsules off the shelves. It was among the first large-scale product recalls in America.

Tylenol, at that time, held about one-third of the US market. In the aftermath, their share fell to eight percent—a drop of more than three-quarters. J&J needed to act decisively to save their business, and they did. All Tylenol capsules (two-part gelatin ovoids containing powdered medicine) were discontinued. (Other manufacturers soon followed suit.)

Tylenol returned to the shelves ten weeks after the recall, as "caplets"—capsule-shaped tablets coated in gelatin and bottled with the now-familiar "tamper-resistant" plastic wrap around the top. Tylenol redeployed with a marketing campaign about product safety. (Partly, that worked because it already had a solid reputation for effectiveness.) They regained their former market share within a year.

Murder and other similar disasters aren't memories that fade quickly. Lighter-than-air ships were a fast-growing transportation model until the Hindenburg disaster—the industry never recovered, and we all know why. J&J overcame an environment of fear by acting with amazing speed and creating a solution so effective that federal legislation now requires some form of tamper-resistant packaging on virtually all consumables.

Conquering your environment often requires you to go out of the box to create things that might initially be viewed as quirky, crazy, or strange. These unique actions help redirect people's attention away from the situation and refocus it on what you're trying to accomplish.

How Bad Do You Want It?

Commitment requires wanting it so badly that you eat, sleep, drink, and breathe it.

You are determined—without any hesitation—that this is going to work, and you are going to bring every resource at your disposal to make it work. There's a measure of controlled obsession in success.

Think of the military's most elite soldiers, the snipers, the behind-the-lines operators. When they know that a certain person is an obstacle to success—if I may put it so delicately—that obstacle must be removed. That person must be taken out of the picture. There is no other option. There have been times, I'm told, that the mission came down to the last man who carried out the mission after the fashion of Japanese *kamikaze* pilots.

I was tempted, at this point, to write "Granted, very few people die trying to get rich," but that isn't always true. In 1848, as the Mexican War concluded, a group of mustered-out soldiers went to work building a mill for John Sutter. The rest is history, but one that rarely mentions how few "struck it rich." Between 1849 and 1855, an estimated 300,000 joined the Gold Rush. Estimates range around ten percent died in the effort due to disease, malnutrition, accidents and, of course, violence. A generation later, thousands more died in similar numbers during the Klondike Gold Rush.

Today, success is less physically deadly, but numerous lesser risks continue. The sixty, seventy, and eighty-hour weeks kill many marriages. Worse than divorce, entrepreneurs become estranged from their children, other relatives, and friends. Is it still success if you have no one to share it with? There are also health risks, such as growing old prematurely with heart disease, dying from stress-induced heart attacks or strokes, because the work schedule precludes eating right and exercising properly. These are real, documented risks.

So, I ask you: are you willing to risk everything and anything to achieve your goal? Because that's often what is required. How bad do you want it?

Part of success lies in analyzing the risks—some of which are beyond what you can imagine as you plan your strategy, while others arise once you're in it up to your eyeballs. Because that does happen. Many times along the path, people find themselves in places they never thought they'd be. Where are you willing to sacrifice to meet your objectives?

Giving Up

Failure is relative. When a project doesn't reach completion, many reasons could underlie that failure.

Many years ago, I bought a house intending to renovate and resell it. For some reason, the locals were not helpful in completing the project—quite the opposite! After getting part-way through the renovation, I found myself alone. I couldn't find the proper contractors to finish the work. The neighbors, I found out, did not want the project to work. (I never found out why.) After I spent $300,000, it became clear the project was over. I was determined to see it through, but I was alone in that. I sold it at a loss of about $115,000. I regret it to this day, but I don't regret walking away—that was necessary. I regret my inability to make the project work.

I'm a perfectionist—defeat isn't fun. Especially, defeat by forces who had no reason to oppose me. After all, was it any of their business? Well, they made it their business. I'll go a step further and recognize that many people, myself included, are tremendously focused on the mantra, "I am a winner, and I have to win. I have to win at everything, and I do, whether it's romance or finance or anything else."

That said, I don't think that defeat is always a negative outcome. It's the intelligent recognition that life is going down a different path from the one you envisioned. I could've fought and I might've won, however, you can get to the point where your win is a loss.

It hurts. It hurts your soul, your spirit, and your mind. Sometimes, you wake up, see the situation, and all you can say is, "I don't believe this. I don't believe I got this far and still couldn't win." That's a key indicator that you can't take defeat well. Sometimes, however, we simply have to bow to the inevitable. That is a fact of life we all have to learn, a vital one. After all, it's been said that we have to know defeat to fully enjoy success.

CHAPTER 8

Putting Skills to Practice

I've written very little over the years—I'm not a writer—but I did put a couple of short pamphlets that I think should be included here. These are two separate lists, so there is some repetition. However, I've reviewed and updated both to ensure they are the best I can make them. I hope you find something useful in them.

8 Steps to Success

1. Have a Vision

The Bible says, *"Where there is no vision, the people perish."*[8]

Stephen Covey, the late time management guru, wrote, "Begin with the End in Mind."[9] Some people refer to this as "reverse engineering"—"This is where we want to be, and this is how we get there."

We could quote a dozen sources, all encouraging you to start your plan by clearly defining what you hope to accomplish. Well, let's keep it simple: If you don't know what you're trying to accomplish, how can you know that you've finished the job?

2. Break the Mission into Components

The ancient question still applies: "How do you eat an elephant? One bite at a time."

Realizing you can't accomplish it all on your own is part of adulthood. Take, for example, a photographer who sells fancy, framed landscapes and still lifes. She does well but even though she's a sole proprietor who takes all the pictures, she will fail as a business without help. She needs a bookkeeper to watch her finances, a camera store for equipment, a gallery to sell her work, a car dealer to get her out into the field to shoot those landscapes, and more.

When we think about dividing the work up, we must think about width and length. We develop a plan dividing the project into steps, stages, or phases—whatever you want to call them: research, development testing, production, marketing, and more. We also divide them into departments: accounting,

---

[8] Proverbs 29:18, King James Version.
[9] Covey, Steven Richards. *The 7 Habits of Highly Effective People*. New York City: Free Press (now an imprint of Simon & Schuster), 1989.

human resources, operations, research, and more. In each phase and department, you need technical experts. Hire or contract with the best people you can find.

3. Understand Obstacles

> No battle plan ever survives first contact with the enemy.
>
> —Helmuth von Moltke the Elder[10]

If you could control everything, your plan would be perfect, simple, and always effective. You can't even control yourself a hundred percent of the time. That's why alternatives are vital—a Plan B, a Plan C, maybe even a Plan Q or Y might be necessary. Don't hesitate to go there if you have to. Likewise, there are probably a million books about planning, project management, and similar topics. Read them! Read a lot of them. They can be useful and help you expand your knowledge base.

Understanding potential obstacles means recognizing where you are and acknowledging that there are things ahead of you that you cannot overcome.

In such cases, your path to success goes around, over, under, or through the obstacle. As Clint Eastwood said, "Improvise, adapt, overcome!"[11]

4. Discipline Yourself to Get Up and Go!

> The man who is tenacious of purpose in a rightful cause is not shaken from his firm resolve by the frenzy

---

[10] A more literal translation is, "No plan of operations extends with any certainty beyond the first contact with the main hostile force." Helmuth Karl Bernhard Graf von Moltke, "On Strategy," quoted in Daniel J. Hughes and Harry Bell, *Moltke on the Art of War: Selected Writings*. New York City: Random House Publishing Group, 1995.

[11] Eastwood, Clint, director. *Heartbreak Ridge*. Malpaso Productions and Warner Bros., 1986.

of his fellow citizens clamoring for what is wrong, or by the tyrant's threatening countenance.

—Horace[12]

Humans tend to be better at planning than executing. Buck that trend. Be the person that always shows up, ready to work, happy to be working, and dedicated to doing your best that day and every day. Earn yourself a reputation like that, and you'll never be unemployed.

And be ready to get knocked over. It happens. So, when it happens, you need the discipline to get back up, go forward, and continue no matter what's going on around and to you.

5. Challenge Yourself and Never Surrender

Sir, I have not yet begun to fight!

—attributed to John Paul Jones

In 1779, Jones, a captain in the young US Navy, took command of USS *Bonhomme Richard*. He sailed to England, where he met a British warship, HMS *Serapis*. In a fierce cannon duel, *Bonhomme Richard* sustained heavy damage and Jones realized that, in a gun-to-gun fight, he was going to lose. According to legend, Capt. Richard Pearson of the *Serapis* called on Jones to surrender. Jones responded with his now-famous defiance. *Bonhomme Richard* then maneuvered alongside *Serapis* and boarded, taking the ship in a fierce hand-to-hand battle.

When you go to work, you'll probably get beaten up. We created a plan, we included alternatives to overcome obstacles, we took a few lumps doing it. That's life—get used to it. You may even get your butt whipped by those obstacles once or twice. Some of us have been pushed into bankruptcy or

---

[12] Quintus Horatius Flaccus, *Odes*, Book 3, Ode 3, line 1, c. 23-13 BC.

some other total disaster. That day is the day you find out what you're made of. (More on this later.)

You have two choices: Stand and deliver or lie down and die.

6. Build Alliances

Giving

We secure our friends not by accepting favors but by doing them.

—Thucydides[13]

Incredibly obvious, is it not? Even so, many people don't do it. When people need help to get things done, help them. One day, you'll be needing help, so why wouldn't you be generous with your influence, skills, or advice? As you think about this question, consider one of the wisest proverbs ever spoken:

You can have everything in life you want, if you will just help enough other people get what they want.

—Zig Ziglar[14]

I believe the greatest happiness comes from helping others achieve success. Are you a good person? Are you trustworthy, loyal, helpful, courteous, kind, and all the other things the Boy Scouts of America used to aspire to be?

That sort of person helps others for no reason beyond, "It's the right thing to do." That attitude and those actions foster a reputation that attracts like-minded individuals to you. People who generously give, the old sage affirmed, are people who abundantly receive. Do we achieve our best successes alone? No,

---

[13] Thucydides. *Funeral Oration of Pericles*, Book 2, Section 37.
[14] Ziglar, Hilary Hinton "Zig". *See You at the Top*. Elmwood, Louisiana: Pelican Publishing Company, 1974.

don't even bother trying. Do good, attract others who do good, create synergy, and watch what happens. You'll be impressed.

Receiving

Allow me to address this subject without sugarcoating—these are hard truths that need to be said:

When speaking publicly, I find many minority people tend to view Anglo-American males as "the enemy." Too many of "my people" refuse to trust or do business with them. Notice, please, that I say, "they refuse," but they would say, "I can't." They're lying to themselves. They can but they choose not to because of prejudice or misinformation. We, African-Americans as a group, and maybe other minorities as well, need to recognize that not everybody who is white is racist and a lot of them are not just willing—they're anxious to help you succeed. They are good people.

Anglo-American men still form the backbone of American business and politics. As I look back on the alliances I've made throughout my life, more Anglo-American men have rallied to my cause than any other group. It was Anglo-American men who so often went to bat for me—they're a major reason why I've gotten where I am.

To the minority entrepreneurs or others who can't bring themselves to cross that line, I'm already ordering flowers for your business' funeral.

7. Recognize Built-in Loses

There are potential losses inherent in every project. Look for them, acknowledge them, and deal with them. Don't pretend it can't happen to you. Some statistics from 2022: Walmart lost $6.1 billion due to retail theft—equivalent to about one percent of Walmart's total revenue that year. Target expected to report losing over $600 million due to theft that year. The average loss per shoplifting incident (among all retailers) is over $500.[15]

Retailers expect those losses, have figured them into their financial plans, and live with them. The cost of making a store theft-proof is higher than what they lose. What type and level of loss will happen to you? No one can predict that, but those losses could be the difference between survival and failure.

Prepare for them.

8. Acknowledge Your Wins

> Celebrate good times, come on!
> Let's celebrate! …
>
> —Kool & The Gang[16]

At regular intervals, you'll reach benchmarks. When you and your people have done well, don't hide the fact. Do something to tell yourself and your people, "You did good!" Celebrating individual and group wins are important—even vital—for group morale, and group morale is vital to your success.

15 Strategic Moves to Reach your Life's Purposes

1. Create Your Objectives

This is number one! I repeat from the previous list: Before you begin, you need to know the final outcome. If you don't, how can you know if you've succeeded or failed?

---

[15] Osborn, Joe. "13 Walmart Theft Statistics You Need To Know," DealAid. org. Toronto, Ontario: Digicove. 2023. https://dealaid.org/data/walmart-theft/, accessed 25 February 2025.

[16] "Celebration," written by Ronald Nathan Bell, Claydes Charles Smith, et al, produced by Eumir Deodato and Kool & the Gang. Hilversum, Netherlands: De-Lite Recorded Sound Corporation (now part of Universal Music Group), released October 1980.

2. Craft Goals

Goals are not simply written—they are crafted like a fine meal or a magnificent painting. When you can explain the vision, you can define how to get there. As we've learned, it is a form of reverse engineering.

1. Visions and goals mean more than change; they mean progress. So, goals must define how you will be more than you are at present.

2. They say, "Go big, or go home!"

3. They must be possible. Stretch a rubber band and it becomes useful; stretch it too far, and it snaps, becoming useless.

4. They must be timely. *"To every thing there is a season, and a time to every purpose under the heaven"*[17]

5. "When we deal in generalities, we shall never succeed. When we deal in specifics, we shall rarely have a failure. When performance is measured and reported, the rate of performance accelerates."[18]

6. "If it isn't written down, it didn't happen" or "A goal not written is only a wish." And, after they're written, share them and be accountable!

---

[17] Ecclesiastes 3:1 (King James Version).
[18] Attributed to English statistician Karl Pearson, quoted, as above, by Thomas Monson, "untitled," *Conference Report*. Salt Lake City: The Church of Jesus Christ of Latter-day Saints, October 1970.

3. Create Blueprints and Follow Them

Make no little plans. They have no magic to stir men's blood and probably will not themselves be realized. Make big plans; aim high in hope and work, remembering that a noble, logical diagram once recorded will never die, but long after we are gone will be a living thing, asserting itself with ever growing insistency.

–Daniel Burnham[19]

4. Create Crucial Associations

Among the obvious "crucial" associations are people you trust to tell you the truth–harsh truths like:

- "This is wrong!"

- "You're overthinking the problem, and you need to back up a little."

- "This isn't worth fighting for."

Most importantly, the person who can say:

- "There's no path to success here; pack it up and go home."

5. Develop Persuasive Strategies

Can you "Fake it 'til you make it"? Here's a slightly tongue-in-cheek idea that sounds crazy, but look at it carefully:

---

[19] Burnham, Daniel H. and Edward H. Bennett. *Plan of Chicago*, 1909. Quoted in *The Electronic Encyclopedia of Chicago*. Chicago: Chicago Historical Society, 2005. http://www.encyclopedia.chicagohistory.org/pages/2396.html#:~:text=Daniel%20Burnham%20is%20perhaps%20best,will%20not%20themselves%20be%20realized, accessed 26 February 2025.

I suggest that the best conman is one who can con himself. Some ideas are so out there, so revolutionary—ideas like every home can have a computer on a desk or every person can have a phone in their pocket—that they sound like fantasy. You need to "con" yourself into believing that it's possible. If you believe it so deeply, everybody else will also believe you eventually.

6. Act Decisively

Dear Pessimist, Optimist, and Realist,

While you three were arguing over whether the glass was half-empty, half-full, or just half a glass, I drank it.

Sincerely, The Opportunist.

—Unknown

There are a thousand ways to say it, so, I'll just say it this way: Get off your butt and do something!

7. Overcome Fear

Fate whispers to the warrior, "You cannot withstand the storm."

The warrior whispers back, "I am the storm."

—Modern Proverb

When I was a kid, I always volunteered to get the mail. Every day, I went, but I had a problem: I had to walk by this dog in the neighbor's yard. I ran past him because I was scared to death of him. One day, I got it into my mind to stop this. So, as I walked past his yard, he ran up to the fence and jumped up against it. I didn't run; I kept walking. Same the next day and the next, until, as I walked by, he just sat there, looking at me. All those years, I ran, until I got tired of running.

Getting tired is the key. As long as you're willing to give into your fear, you will.

That which doesn't kill me ... had better run!

– an (alleged) Old Viking Proverb

8. Exploit Opportunity or Opportunities

Opportunity is missed by most people because it is dressed in overalls and looks like work.

–Thomas Alva Edison[20]

One example: Shortly after moving to New York City, I attended an event at The Museum of Modern Art, known in the city as "the MoMA." By chance, I met a woman whose family were major players in New York real estate. I got bold and started talking business with her and, before long, I was helping her invest her money. Neither of us was there to do business nor did we expect to meet the other. Frankly, I probably should've kept my mouth shut, since most people would say that a newcomer had no business hitting up one of the major players.

Well, I didn't.

9. Maximize Resources Both Large and Small

When I was in real estate, I had a huge electronic library of historical data–newspapers and magazines–all the way back to the turn of the 20th Century. It's public info, but most people don't know about it. I also had a girlfriend at that time in a real estate business broker's office. She provided me with ownership info on all the buildings on each block in the city. I knew who to deal with and using my electronic database, I had access to a lot of info about them. I used both extensively and to great profit.

---

[20] Thomas Edison, quoted in John Mason. *An Enemy Called Average*. Tulsa, OK: Harrison House Inc, 1990.

10. Leverage Your Strength or Strengths

I know a gal who works as a Spanish-to-English translator for medical practices. Most of the time, she works as an esthetician—she does facials and advises clients on makeup, skin & haircare, and stuff like that. But, unlike most people in her neighborhood, she speaks excellent Spanish, offers that service to health clinics and others, and gets paid well for that work. She saw a need and leveraged a strength which others didn't have into a solution and a profit.

11. Practice and Repeat

> What is the real difference between a professional and an amateur?
>
> An amateur practices until he can do a thing right, a professional until he can't do it wrong.
>
> –Sir Percy Carter Buck[21]

They say it takes 10,000 hours of effort to become an expert.

The clock is ticking—you'd better get started.

12. Create Positive Reinforcement

> 'Tis not in mortals to command success,
>
> But we'll do more, Sempronius, we'll deserve it![22]

Gather people who are focused on solutions instead of problems. If you have five people in your innermost circle who are broke, you need to change that before you become the sixth! If you have five people who think and are proactively working toward success, your chances of success increase dramatically.

[21] Buck, Sir Percy Carter. *Psychology for Musicians*. London: Oxford University Press, 1944.
[22] Addison, Joseph. *Cato*, Act I, Scene 2, 1713.

13. Understand Yourself

> The vision that you glorify in your mind, the ideal that you enthrone in your heart—this you will build your life by, and this you will become.
>
> —James Allen[23]

It doesn't come naturally; self-awareness takes work. But it is the first step in controlling yourself, and self-control is a key to success. Ask yourself: "Why do I react to certain things the way I do?" "What exhausts me?" "What really excites me?" "What frustrates me?" "What do I value most—what will I drop everything to take care of?" "Who do I most admire?"

There is a boatload of personality tests available on the internet. I don't know how useful they are, but if you take several and they all end up with similar results, you are definitely on to something. You can also ask those in your inner circle, those you trust without question or hesitation, and, most certainly, your spouse or partner.

14. Understand Others

> I make progress by having people around me who are smarter than I am and listening to them. And I assume that everyone is smarter about something than I am.
>
> —attributed to Henry John Kaiser[24]

An interesting story:

> "I wasn't so young as not to know that, since I had undertaken a profession, I had better try to understand it." That he was earnest about this, he proceeded to prove in a rather curious manner; he "had one of the privates weighed in his clothes only, and then with all his arms,

---

[23] Allen, James. "Visions and Ideals," *As A Man Thinketh*, 1903.
[24] Oft quoted on the internet.

accouterments and kit in full marching order." Obviously, the reason for this was to find out how much a man had to carry on active service and what proportion it bore to his own weight. ... From this little episode, we may draw two deductions, not very favorable to the British Army of that time. In the first place, the weight to be carried by a soldier should have been laid down in Field Service Regulations; in the second place, no officer should command men until he has drilled and marched as they have to do wearing their equipment. But the fact that an Ensign, not yet eighteen, with only a few days' service should have seen the necessity for this knowledge is significant. It showed a recognition of the importance of the private soldier very rare in those days.

–Richard Aldington[25]

The young ensign referred to was Arthur Wellesley, a younger son of a minor noble in Britain. This rare combination of insight and intelligent inquiry brought him tremendous success as a soldier. Success so rare that only two men in the first half of the 19th Century stand atop the list of military geniuses–the Emperor Napoleon and young Arthur, later the Duke of Wellington.

"The importance of the private soldier" is an overlooked part of success. In general terms, it is the power of a single individual, whether they work on the shop floor or in the executive suite, to make or break a project. So, know them well enough to get them doing what they're best at.

15. Know When to Engage and You'll Miss No Opportunities

When God (or the universe, fate, karma–whatever you choose to call it) speaks, listen!

---

[25] Aldington, Edward Godfree. *The Duke: Being an Account of the Life and Achievements of Arthur Wellesley, 1st Duke of Wellington.* New York: Viking Press, 1943.

If you truly know yourself and have a firm vision of what you want your life to be, your subconscious activates a radar-like system that'll "ping" on opportunities. We'll never get them all, but when all of the ideas in this book take firm root in your psyche profile, the odds that you'll hear something and say, "Oh, I can make that work for me" will be high.

And you will.

CHAPTER 9

Mentality

My father was the type of guy who, when I did something wrong enough to attract what I'll call "official attention," left me in jail at the end of the day.

I learned very quickly that jail is not the place I want to be. Much of life's success or failure is based on your mentality or mindset. Where your mind is, your body inevitably follows. Fortunately, you can teach, train, or retrain your mind to go where you want to be.

The Loser-Outlook

You won't know your highest potential until you face the most challenging moment in your life.

One of the things that I have not touched upon heavily is losing. Every one of us is "the loser" at some point and only a fool thinks otherwise. How we deal with failure is as important, if not more so, than how we deal with success. Here's the question: Are you going to be the loser of the moment or are you going to adopt the lifestyle of the loser?

Our lifestyle, that is, the attitude with which we look at our life at present and our life to come, defines our potential for success. Someone with a loser-outlook has no goals or reason to hope because they "know" that whatever they do will fail. Someone with a winner-outlook sets goals because they know there will be small failures on the road to big success but they carry the discipline and vision to continue on to that success.

Let's take an all-too-common example—mental health. I know a guy who suffers from ADHD, autism, and chronic clinical depression. As a result, he didn't relate well to "normal" people. (In fact, at times, he related very badly to other people.) He wasn't diagnosed until middle age, meaning, he didn't understand his problem. Because of this, he couldn't deal effectively with that problem. He lost jobs and friends, and he had all sorts of other problems. In many respects, and in the opinions of many who knew him, he was a loser. He actually considered suicide as a viable option.

So, what did he do when, finally, he was diagnosed? He could've given up on having good relationships. He could've simply kept on the way he'd been going, adopting the loser-outlook. He didn't. He began to learn workarounds for his conditions. Today, he watches himself, listening to his voice for stress indicators. He knows his triggers and avoids them. He still has problems but he's so much better at dealing with them than he was as a young man that most people remain completely unaware of what he deals with on a daily basis unless he tells them. He's adopted the winner-outlook.

If you're looking for advice, you're reading the wrong book. I'm not a mental health expert, and I don't know the details of your situation. I can only look at my situation and share my experiences with the hope that some of mine are similar enough to yours that you'll get a hint on how to deal with yours, but it's only a hint. If you see something in yourself that stumps you, my best advice is to find professional help. There was, once upon a time, a terrible stigma about mental health counselling. Those days are long gone, and you cheat yourself if you see a need and don't take advantage of the help that's available.

And that goes for your physical health, business health, financial health, spiritual health, emotional health, familial relationships, romantic relationships, you name it. If you're feeling like a loser, you're wrong; you're probably no better or worse off than the rest of us. But you could be better—and there is no shame in getting help to get better. It's the responsible, adult move. Needing help, having it available, and not getting it should be the disgrace.

Rock Bottom

Take "the loser" scenario to its worst-case scenario: your career's off, your family's off, your whole life, it seems, has gone off the rails. You feel like life could not possibly get worse.

"I'm at the bottom," you say to yourself, and "I've fallen, and I can't get up."

If that's what you really said, I have good news.

You're Wrong

You should've said, "I'm at the bottom. I need to jumpstart my life." That's recognition that your life has come completely apart but the situation is not hopeless. You can recover or start over.

You should've also said, "I've fallen, and I can't get up on my own." That's recognition that you need help–you just have to find the people who can give the help you need.

These are the key differences between the loser-outlook and the winner-outlook.

However, even recognizing these important truths, we might find ourselves in what I call a **YOYO** moment. It's that moment when you look around and you can't see any help. You're sure no help is coming; that moment when you're sure **Y**ou're **O**n **Y**our **O**wn.

I have more good news.

You're Wrong Again

You are never on your own. I know many of you are not religious, maybe you're even convinced God doesn't exist. I respectfully disagree. I believe God is always there, even when you're sure He isn't.

He can turn any situation into a positive experience. You may have to endure some hard times. Your situation might appear so harsh that it looks hopeless. It might even look like it's getting worse before it gets better. You might have to conquer an openly hostile environment. It may take years to achieve the victory. You might not be able to see the end of the tunnel or its light until you're almost there.

But, if you'll follow where God (the universe, karma, fate–whatever you choose to call it) guides you, there's a potential win in whatever condition you're stuck in. A final story from Coach:

Some years ago, a friend of mine came to me with a project. This project was big, it could have made life better for thousands of people and their families. Had it been successful, I would've retired a wealthy man years ago, but the project leader died of cancer before the financing was firmly set. Despite many efforts to keep it going, the whole thing fell apart.

I'd spent a lot of time and effort getting my part of the project set up. When I couldn't get paid for what I'd done, I lost my business, and just about everything else. Sold my car and other things to pay my rent and, when I ran out of stuff to sell, I lost my home. I was taken in by a college friend, ended up living in a trailer in his backyard for an uncomfortably long time.

I felt like I was totally on my own, like God had abandoned me or exiled me or something equally horrible. For months, I saw nothing positive and no way to fix my situation. Then, my niece sent me a message saying she and her husband wanted to buy me a DNA test. Not anything I wanted at that moment, but I said yes. When the results arrived, I went to the company's website to see the results. Then, out of curiosity, I went wandering around their site to see what else I could see.

I saw almost nothing on my father's family. So, I set up a tree and started researching. Over the next many months, I spent a good part of my free time each day job hunting, and was rewarded with some temp jobs, but I also found myself with a lot of time between jobs. On such days, I hunted relatives. Ten years later, I have two family trees, for dad's mother and for his father, totaling over 30,000 people.

Eventually, I found a full-time job, so my research has slowed down, but I jokingly claim to be the world's leading expert on dad's family because FamilySearch.org, Ancestry.com, and other genealogy sites now have dozens of trees which include my family data. By my estimation, at least eighty percent of what they contain is data based on my work, much of it is copied directly from my trees.

I would never suggest God destroyed my professional life so I could take up this cause. That said, as a freelance writer, I'd become a skilled internet researcher. I think He might've taken a personal disaster and nudged me into creating a valuable experience for myself and thousands of others, making it possible for them—and for me—to discover our family roots and to know, a little better, who we are.

Looking back, it wasn't a fun experience, I'll never say it was. However, if there's something on the other side of death, when I cross over and meet the people I've learned about, I've no doubt I'll feel very lucky to have had that experience.

I have to agree, you're never on your own. Whatever disaster you find yourself in, it will be just a short moment in eternity, and things will, most of the time, get better. God can make them good, in His own time and His own way.

Just remember some old proverbs: "Fate doesn't decide, you do!" "We learn to walk by stumbling." And, of course, "He who laughs last, laughs best." So, hang in there, a reason to laugh is out there, waiting for you to find it.

The Winner-Outlook

Discipline vs. Motivation

I'm guessing you wake up some days and you are entirely unmotivated to get out of bed. So does everybody else on some days. How do you develop the discipline to overcome that lack of motivation?

This, too, is a mentality. I lie there and I remind myself that help is not coming. At least, it shouldn't come when I can do it on my own. Sooner or later, you have to realize that adulthood means I have no other viable choice than to do what it takes to care for myself and my family. I've got to man up–adapt, innovate, overcome. I must do what needs to be done because no one else will. That's the key–choice!

I learned this very young, when my dad said to me:

> You know what, son? I had a headache for 34 years. I had migraines. Do you think I wanted to go to work on even a single day with a migraine? There was no choice. There were people to be fed, house payments to be made, and on and on. Would I prefer to leave and let be it and just forget about life? Sure, but the bottom line of it is, responsibilities eliminate your choices. There is no other option for a real man.

A preacher once said, "You have free agency only until you use it. Once you make a choice, you are locked into the consequences of those choices."

That is life.

Destiny

Traditionally, people use it to describe the "only-case scenario," something unchangeable. I don't buy it. I also don't believe, "We make our own destiny," any more than I believe those who tell me, "If you can conceive it, you can achieve it." We can conceive anything, but we are all limited by our weaknesses.

Earlier, I wrote an add-on to, "Shoot for the stars, you may land on the roof. Shoot for the roof, you may land in the trash can." I added, "Shoot for the stars, you might just reach them." When you make the most of your strengths and work within or around your weaknesses, then and only then, can you reach the stars—your "best-case scenario." I call that "your first, best destiny."

Some people set out to change the world. A few of them succeed. I'm not too worried about that because I'm not Thomas Edison or Albert Einstein or Elon Musk. I don't want to (nor do I ever expect to) change the world. I'm not too interested in doing something nobody's ever done before. The key performance indicator for me is, "Am I fulfilling my destiny? Am I doing the best that I can do?"

By the way, there will be days when you give a half-hearted effort on something. Congratulations, you're human. Come back tomorrow and do better.

If It's Not in the Cards, Do Something Else

Sometimes, circumstances prevent you from moving in the direction you want to go. You can stop and cry about how unfair the world is (re-read the part about the loser-outlook) or you can go with the flow.

At one point in life, I wanted to be a banker. To do that, to be really successful, I needed a graduate degree like an MBA. Why didn't it work out for me? Two reasons:

First, because the money wasn't there at the time. There was no financial help available from my parents, and my prospects for scholarships were dim.

Second, while I researched scholarships and academic requirements, I didn't feel like I wanted to sit down for two, maybe four, years—basically wasting a lot of time listening to monetary theory and talking about monetary policy. I realized that I want to be moving, to be in the thick of things. I wanted to make deals right then.

Why? What was it about being a banker that appealed to me?

Good news, I won't say I wanted to play with other people's money—that's too cliché.

No, no, no, it was the power of it that I wanted. Somebody once said something like, "Give me not who runs the country, but give me who has the money." I wanted to be that guy. Bankers have power—they are financing, they're creating things, they can do a lot to build their communities up. I realized that I didn't have to be a banker to do that. If I could make deals with people who had money, I could make as much difference as a banker. (I later learned that I could do it with a lot less red tape, which still thrills me today.)

So, then, it was a matter of figuring out how to be creative in real estate. (That was the best way, I thought, to do something good for my neighborhood.) How to turn the neighborhood around and make something out of nothing, you know, how do you make deals? How do you convince someone that you're a good investment risk or a good bet?

Well, I knew something about women—not much more than any man, but something important: They date you because they find you charming.

I applied that idea to real estate. I was charming, and eventually, I became charming enough to sell snow to an Eskimo. Those first small deals were successful and, having gained a reputation for success, I was able to charm people into loaning me more money to make a bigger deal, and on and on.

To sum up, my success was a product of a disciplined and motivated mentality. I knew my market, that is, what my potential customers needed in the way of housing. I knew the audience, that is, my potential investors. I learned their needs, how to approach them, and how to take advantage of my opportunities— building alliances and covering the whole nine yards that I've been talking about. There is some natural talent, I assume, but most of it is skill I developed through years of practice: if you're going after a certain type of person to get an investment (or take part in almost any other type of project), you've simply got to know what they want to get out of that investment then you have to convince them that you can deliver.

Balance

One final note that is important: We all have several different things going on in our lives. We need to focus on each of them in their turn—your job, family, personal health, relationships with friends and relatives, community activities, etc. Each requires and deserves your full attention at times.

You should be aware of them at all times because emergencies arise, and people trust you to have their back at such times. Maintaining balance means you give each thing its due, moving toward peak performance in each responsibility. A simple example: after a bad day in business, go sweat it out at the gym and relieve the stress so you can go home and have a good evening with your family.

Another example: the spouse and kids know you'll have to work sixty-plus hours a week during tax time if you're an accountant. They don't resent you for that time away if they know you're taking time off as soon as tax season is over and school's out and the whole family is going to their favorite play place to ignore the rest of the world for a week or two.

Keep an eye on each part of your life, anticipate problems, plan for them, give each of them the time they deserve, give each the precision of your best work, and synchronize all the aspects to work together.

If you can do that, you'll do your best for each part of your life.

Do you want to be your own enlightened coach? Scan the QR code to learn more.

Appendix: Connect with Me

Website:	Dariuswrites.com
Email:	Darius@dariusross.com
Instagram:	@Darreexec
X:	@dacatman
Facebook:	Facebook.com/dariusaross1

Author Bio

Darius Ross is a distinguished serial entrepreneur and a true survivor who has faced and overcome myriad of challenges. His journey from homelessness to urban warfare has equipped him with unparalleled tactical and strategic skills, which he now leverages to guide both high-net-worth individuals and everyday entrepreneurs toward success. Ross's consulting practice is renowned for its tailored approach, catering to a diverse clientele ranging from families with substantial assets to aspiring business owners.

Ross is a noted podcast guest and political and economic pundit, frequently sharing his insights on various platforms. He is a renowned speaker who has been invited to speak at numerous prestigious events. As an accomplished author, Ross has written seven influential books on a range of topics. His works include *Dating at 50 Plus: Parts 1 and 2—Seeking Romance After Your Fairy Tale Youth*, *TPS (Timing, Synchronicity, and Precision)*, *25 Mental Phrases to Memorize for Your Success*, and *PPP (Prepare, Participate, and Profit): Your Rx for Post-COVID Multifamily Real Estate Investing*. These publications reflect his diverse expertise and his commitment to sharing knowledge that empowers others to succeed in both personal and professional life.

Ross serves as an advisor to high-net-worth individuals and ultra-high-net-worth families, managing assets ranging from fifty million dollars to more than one trillion dollars. He is also an angel investor in over 750 to 1,000 companies, spanning industries from artificial intelligence and technology software to medical and pharmaceutical sectors, with a total asset base of one hundred billion dollars. Additionally, Ross is a limited partner in a private partnership group that controls more than one hundred thousand multifamily apartment units.

Currently, Ross is spearheading the creation of a Master Partnership focused on acquiring real estate resources and infrastructure-based companies. His ambitious goal is to acquire more than one thousand companies globally, developing a one hundred trillion dollar infrastructure holding group.

For more information, visit his website at dariuswrites.com or contact him at drspktoyou@yahoo.com or darius@dariusross.com.

www.ingramcontent.com/pod-product-compliance
Lightning Source LLC
Chambersburg PA
CBHW021119130626
46554CB00002B/772